T0293645

PRAISE FOR *DIGITAL TALENT*

In a year that combined a continuation of the COVID-19 pandemic and a reset of the employee experience dubbed 'The Great Resignation' this book is an in-depth analysis of how the world of talent acquisition has to adapt at pace to attract, engage and retain digital talent. Meticulously researched with real life case studies, this book is a must-read for every HR leader tasked with transforming their organization's talent offering.

Charu Malhotra – Head of Global Talent Marketing, PA Consulting

Few in the staffing industry have the experience, access and authority to be able to write a book like this. *Digital Talent* covers topical urgencies like diversity and inclusion, digital leadership, shift to remote, evolution of HR technology and the changing relationship we have with work. We are fortunate that Mervyn Dinnen and Matt Alder – two veterans of the industry who each independently have forged unique paths as analysts and commentators – can collaborate so successfully in pulling together the trends which are shaping the world of work today. An essential read.

Hung Lee – Curator, Recruiting Brainfood

This book is a gem – summarizing a wide range of data into a highly readable and useful book. Matt and Mervyn have provided the HR and talent acquisition profession with an outstanding overview of the challenges and opportunities that define this century as well as insight into how to adapt. Highly recommended.

Kevin Wheeler – Founder, The Future of Talent Institute

Digital Talent covers an incredible range of areas in a consistently accessible and rich way. Any organization or practitioner interested in navigating through the fog of hype around the implications of an ever-increasing digital focus will find this book invaluable, both as a gateway and a guide. Whether it is busting myths about millennials or looking at the changing nature of the functions driving progress, there is a wealth smartly positioned thinking and provocation in its pages.
David D'Souza – Membership Director, CIPD

I am absolutely delighted that our Institute's research has helped with the research for *Digital Talent*. There has never been a more important time for modern leaders to embrace digital transformation and people centric technology in connecting their people to purpose, to accomplishment and to one another.
Robert Ordever – Managing Director, OC Tanner Europe

Digital Talent makes a well-researched and eloquent case for businesses to radically change their thinking around talent acquisition, performance enablement and leadership. It covers all aspects of the talent journey and creates a compelling vision for the transformation of the future workplace. This book is an urgent wake-up call for HR and business leaders everywhere.
Lucinda Carney – CEO and Founder, Actus Software

Yet another barnstorming book from Mervyn and Matt, this time about digital talent. The book is a blend of insight, good ideas and practical solutions to a challenge most organizations are struggling with: how do we attract, hire and retain the digital capability we need to be successful? This really is a must-read for all those dealing with this business critical issue.
Kevin Green – Chief People Officer, First Bus PLC and best-selling author of *Competitive People Strategy*

Digital Talent

*Find, recruit and retain the people your business
needs in a world of digital transformation*

Matt Alder
Mervyn Dinnen

KoganPage

Publisher's note

Every possible effort has been made to ensure that the information contained in this book is accurate at the time of going to press, and the publishers and authors cannot accept responsibility for any errors or omissions, however caused. No responsibility for loss or damage occasioned to any person acting, or refraining from action, as a result of the material in this publication can be accepted by the editor, the publisher or the author.

First published in Great Britain and the United States in 2022 by Kogan Page Limited

2nd Floor, 45 Gee Street	8 W 38th Street, Suite 902	4737/23 Ansari Road
London	New York, NY 10018	Daryaganj
EC1V 3RS	USA	New Delhi 110002
United Kingdom		India

www.koganpage.com

Kogan Page books are printed on paper from sustainable forests.

ISBNs

Hardback   978 1 7896 6019 7
Paperback   978 0 7494 9095 9
Ebook   978 0 7494 9165 9

British Library Cataloguing-in-Publication Data

A CIP record for this book is available from the British Library.

Library of Congress Control Number

2021058573

Typeset by Integra Software Services, Pondicherry
Print production managed by Jellyfish
Printed and bound by CPI Group (UK) Ltd, Croydon CR0 4YY

CONTENTS

ABOUT THIS BOOK

This book is for business, talent and HR leaders who are seeking to understand the wider landscape around shortages in digital skills and put strategies in place for their organizations to have the talent they need for digital transformation. Each chapter explores a different aspect of acquiring, developing and retaining digital talent to help build a picture of the challenges employers are facing, how they are being solved now and how they will be solved in the future.

In the first part of the book, we will take a deep dive into the talent challenges of the digital economy, expanding on many of the themes discussed in the introduction and looking at the role HR needs to play in digital transformation. We will also look at the innovative approaches that are being used to recruit and upskill talent.

Next, we will cover all aspects of the digital workplace, including employee experience, leadership and technology, as well as explore how employers are actively seeking to solve the diversity issues that are prevalent in the digital sector.

Finally, we will consider the future and likely impact of AI and automation and draw the book to its conclusion by presenting a strategic model that employers can follow to attract, train and retain the digital talent they need to thrive both now and in the future.

ACKNOWLEDGEMENTS

Writing a book like this always relies on the insights and experiences of many brilliant people. We would like to say a massive thank you to everyone who has directly contributed to or helped us with this book. In particular, special thanks go to:

Rory Sutherland, Hung Lee, Kevin Wheeler, Bret Putter, Jackie Glen, Charu Malhotra, Anna Chalon, Rachel Hirsch, Amanda Kirby, Theo Smith, Megan Butler, Jon Krohn, Mahe Bayireddi, Lisa Henderson, Rebecca Seal, Neil Morrison, Tom Goodwin, Tami Rosen, James Uffindell, Tim Pröhm, George LaRocque, Tim Sackett, Ken Ward, Matt Buckland, Sinead Bunting, Joshua Secrest, James Saunders, Kristina Iniguez, Sam Whiteman, Tobias Gunkel, Lucinda Carney, David Wilson, Madeline Laurano, Kevin Grossman, Ben Eubanks, Stacia Sherman Garr, Trish McFarlane, Steve Boese, Robert Ordever, James Humpoletz, David Sturt, Eric Mosley, Derek Irvine, Peter Gold, David D'Souza, Emma Parry, Josh Bersin, Jason Averbook and Ray Alder.

Also a huge thank you to Anne-Marie Heeney, Stephen Dunnell, Lucy Carter and everyone at Kogan Page for their amazing support and patience.

Finally and most importantly we'd like to thank our families, without whom this book would have never been written. Thank you Fiona, Alex, Karen and Max for your incredible support and understanding.

Introduction

Talent transformation

It was one minute to midnight in Auckland, the world held its breath and watched, waiting for the start of a technological Armageddon that could see aeroplanes fall out of the sky, food distribution disrupted and the end of business as usual in every major economy. The threat was so great that people had stockpiled food and water and, in some cases, barricaded themselves into shelters anticipating riots and chaos. The clock ticked past midnight, then the explosions started. The initial cracks and bangs took place over the harbour, as 2000 began in the industrialized world. The explosions were from lavish firework displays, which would be reciprocated all over the globe during the following 24 hours. But it wasn't the fireworks that people were frightened of. It was the Armageddon that they had been warned would be unleashed by the so-called 'Millennium Bug', or Y2K to use its popular abbreviation.

In a time before smartphones, tablets and social media, when many organizations were still trying to decide if they needed to use electronic mail, or even have a website at all, the belief was that the technology that already existed would bring catastrophe to the industrialized world.

The millennium bug was a date-based software glitch that could potentially have led to the failure of computer systems. Its origins could be traced back to the 1950s and 1960s when, to save the minimal memory space that was then available, the software engineers of the time abbreviated the year when writing in dates to its last two numerals. This meant that when the year rolled over from 1999 to 2000, the affected systems would presume it was 1900, causing an enormous potential for shutdowns and critical errors. The consequences were as wide-ranging as they were terrifying. It was predicted that banking systems would cease to operate, air traffic control systems would fail, nuclear power plants would go into meltdown, and vital supply chains would shut down. There were also an estimated seven billion embedded chips that could be affected with dire consequences for medical equipment, temperature control systems in buildings and even the safe operation of lifts. Although the millennium bug had been identified decades before, the world only really started waking up to its potentially catastrophic consequences in the 1990s, but even then, it was still a slow realization. According to Professor Martyn Thomas,[1] a world-renowned expert in software engineering and cybersecurity and an authority on the millennium bug, by 1995 only 8% of UK companies had assessed the risk of the millennium bug to their business. Awareness accelerated over the next five years reaching a crescendo of media-fuelled hysteria in 1999 that had the world deeply worried about the continuation of normal life as we knew it at one minute past minute on millennium night.

This acceleration in awareness during the late 1990s was driven by several things, but two key factors made the world sit up and take notice. The first of these was a coordinated global response from governments. The seriousness and urgency with which the US government treated the situation are clearly illustrated in a speech the then-president Bill Clinton gave at The National Academy of Sciences in July 1998 to underline the preparations that the US government were making:

> It is a complex task that requires us all to work together... I set a government-wide goal of full compliance by March of 1999... The American people have a right to expect uninterrupted service from [the] government, and I expect them to deliver.[2]

The response from other governments was equally robust. In the UK, for example, the government set up Action 2000, which regularly published warnings and advice to both businesses and the general public to ensure that everyone was fully prepared for what was to come.

In his 2017 lecture, 'What Really Happened in Y2K', Martyn Thomas emphasized that the millennium bug was a business problem rather than a technological one. It was all very well for governments to be prepared, but if businesses didn't follow suit, then there was no chance of avoiding a millennium Armageddon. It is fair to say that companies only tend to act when they can clearly understand the consequences on their bottom line, and the millennium bug came sharply into focus when the world's big audit firms announced that they would refuse to sign off the accounts of companies that could not demonstrate Y2K compliance. The consequences were now clear and were something that companies could not now buy insurance to protect themselves against; their long-term survival now depended on them taking action to solve the problem. So how was the problem solved and a seemingly inevitable catastrophe avoided? The good news about the millennium bug was that the problem was easy to understand and was eminently fixable. The bad news was the sheer amount of work it would take to do this. Unsurprisingly then, the 1990s saw the biggest ever mobilization of software professionals in history and a vast number of errors were found and fixed. While software automation was a contributing factor to solving the problem, it was the mobilization of specialist talent that was crucial. The scale of the issue and its unnegotiable deadline created critical skill shortages, particularly with people who had experience in legacy programming languages such as COBOL that a lot of software was written in. This led to both wage inflation and attractive financial incentives being used to tempt a lot of older programmers out of retirement to update code they had written, sometimes many decades earlier. Martyn Thomas identifies examples of the potential catastrophic issues resolved before the millennium eve, which included problems with the UK's anti-aircraft missile system, several nuclear power plants, BP's offshore platforms and 1.3 million Visa payment machines.

Inevitably, not every single bug was found; bills, court summons and birth certificates were sent out in various countries during

January 2000 dated 1900, there were power cuts in Hawaii and some UK credit card transactions failed. However, the massive global effort to fix the bug was a resounding success and the dystopian vision of a millennium Armageddon remained in the realms of media fantasy. As Paddy Tipping, then UK 'Minister for The Millennium Bug' said in an interview a few years later:

> The result was never going to be the catastrophe some predicted... We could see that there hadn't really been any problems in Australia or the Middle East already. We were never in crisis mode. It was a case of a job well done.[3]

This 'job well done' didn't come cheaply though: the estimated global cost of preventing the millennium bug ran into hundreds of billions of dollars. The lack of actual disruption caused has also subsequently led to claims that Y2K was a hoax, but as Dale Vecchio, research director at Gartner Group says:

> People didn't throw 300 billion to 600 billion dollars, Gartner Group's estimate of the total Y2K spending, to fix a problem that didn't exist. People spent [$]300 billion to [$]600 billion fixing it, and that's why nothing happened.[4]

The millennium bug was a wake-up call for the world in more ways than one. In addition to a catastrophe avoided, it made governments and businesses realize just how much they relied on computers and took their normal functioning for granted. The work to solve the millennium bug mapped the interconnectedness of systems in a way that had never been done before and in so doing helped secure the foundations of the technology-driven world we live in today. It also led to a significant upgrade in systems, a new profile for technology within organizations and the inclusion of a chief technology officer on many boards to ensure a proper strategic approach to technology.

This time things are different

So why are we starting a modern business book with a description of events that happened over 20 years ago? In the 1990s the relentless approach of New Year's day 2000 highlighted the importance of acquiring and retaining the right digital talent. Tempting people back from retirement or aggressively headhunting them from competitors could only go so far, and the urgency of the talent problem saw companies looking for more creative solutions that had far-reaching consequences. One example here was the emergence of outsourcing on an industrial scale; in 1998, 40% of the revenue for the Indian software industry came from exporting Y2K services and established it as a dominant global technology force for the decades to come.[5] Fast forward two decades and we find ourselves living in another era where access to the right kind of talent is a make-or-break situation for both companies and employers alike. Once more, companies are looking for creative solutions as critical skills' shortages are holding back growth, and, in some cases, threatening their very survival.

In the two decades since the millennium bug struck fear into the hearts of governments and businesses, digital technology has developed and disrupted everything about the way we live at an unprecedented speed. When exploring the developments that have got us to our current point, it is tempting to categorize them into specific trends. While this is an oversimplification of what has been a very broad and ongoing revolution, it does provide an understandably holistic view that helps makes sense of where we are and where we are going.

In the context of this simplistic view, it is possible to see the millennium as a pivotal point where changes, that were already underway, accelerated as a result of the focus that was put on technology in the closing years of the twentieth century. The growing availability of affordable internet connectivity drove the dot com boom, which ran roughly from 1995 to the middle of 2000. Investors giddy on the business potential of this new medium poured billions of dollars into fresh start-up technology companies that were promising to change the world. Unsurprisingly the reality didn't live up to the hype, and many of these businesses disappeared almost as quickly as they had started when the investor optimism dried up and the bubble burst.

However, while the timescales were wrong, the promises made were right and from about 2002 onwards our next trend, the e-commerce revolution, really started to take hold. Whole industries were disrupted as the way we shopped was changed forever. Fast forward to 2020, and nearly 18% of all worldwide retail sales were via e-commerce, a figure set to rise to 21.8% by 2025.[6] While the world was focusing on the brave new world of e-commerce, the launch of two new websites, which would play a vital role in our next significant digital trend went almost unnoticed. In December 2002, Reid Hoffman, a former executive vice president at PayPal, one of the early winners in the e-commerce revolution, founded LinkedIn as a way of making networking easier for professionals. Fourteen months later in February 2004 Mark Zuckerberg launched what was then called The Facebook with similar aims but for a student audience. Despite their under-the radar-starts, by 2009 both these sites were leading players in a social media revolution that has been relentless in its growth, continually gaining both users and an increasing influence over our lives.

In the latter part of 2021, LinkedIn boasted 740 million users[7] while Facebook had 2.89 billion monthly active users[8] (not counting the additional reach the company gets from its ownership of Instagram and WhatsApp). If e-commerce has changed the way we shop, social media has changed the way we do pretty much everything else.

Fuelling the fire of social media growth was the smartphone revolution, a trend brought to the mainstream when Apple launched the iPhone on 29 June 2007. Mobile phones were already becoming ubiquitous by this point but by adding internet access and launching the App Store, Apple took things to a whole new level.

The digitization of content, media and entertainment has been another huge trend. Spotify, Pandora and Apple Music have effectively ended the physical ownership of music for most people. The popularity of video streaming is also exploding; Netflix alone had amassed 209 million paying subscribers by mid-2021.[9]

The trends of disruption keep coming and accelerating to an even faster pace. Automation and artificial intelligence are promising to unlock innovations a science fiction writer could have only dreamed of 20 years ago and augmented and virtual reality are starting to even change the way we look at the world itself.

Other key developments include the rise of cloud computing, the power of Big Data, the development of Blockchain and Crypto currencies as well the inventions of the self-driving car and the reusable space rocket. This all serves to illustrate though just how momentous the last two decades have been and underline the massive era of change we are currently living through.

The global COVID-19 pandemic has driven a quantum leap in digital transformation with many companies forced to go digital in a matter of days. McKinsey's estimate[10] that the pandemic has accelerated digital transformation by seven years and the UK Consumer Digital Index recently reported that five years' worth of progress was made in digital engagement during the 2020 UK lockdown.[11]

Each stage of ongoing digital disruption has brought its own talent demands, but skill shortages in the digital sphere have been news ever since the mid-1990s. However, we would argue that we are now at a millennium bug style pivotal point when it comes to talent. What we are seeing now is the digitalization of everything and the need for every company to be digital in some way. Digital transformation is the only way that companies can survive and thrive in the years to come. The world has changed, and businesses must change if they want to remain part of it.

As Tom Goodwin, the executive vice president of innovation at Zenith says in his book *Digital Darwinism:* 'The world's best candle-makers continually made better candles, but they never invented the lightbulb. Today companies need to leap to new business models and rethink fundamentals and what they stand for, not slowly tweak what has worked before.'[12]

The pressure on companies to get digital transformation right is immense. This is a winner takes all disruption with successful companies winning big and those that fail to adapt often going out of business. We only have to go to the UK high street to see the brutal reality of this. During 2018, a plethora of household name retailers including HMV, House of Fraser, Maplin, Debenhams and Mothercare either closed shops, were acquired on the verge of administration or disappeared altogether. All of them are facing severe pressure from their e-commerce rivals; Amazon is currently making around $7 billion in profits every quarter.

But this all goes a lot deeper than a simple increase in competition. Amazon are not just a traditional competitor to the high street, they are changing the way consumers behave. Amazon now carries over 500 million different products, most of which can be delivered the next day. Back in the early 2000s when Amazon was just an online bookshop, this kind of reach and coverage would have been considered not just unachievable but something consumers wouldn't want. The received wisdom was that shoppers preferred the experience and tactile hands-on nature of the high street or shopping centre. This received wisdom was wrong.

A dramatic transformation is also being seen in other sectors and notably so in film, TV and music. Netflix has gone from a company that buried Blockbuster videos by posting DVDs online to one that spent $17 billion on original programming in 2021. Netflix's box set approach to content has changed the way we consume film and TV forever, forcing more traditional providers to follow their strategy. Spotify is doing something similar in the world of music. Its 165 million subscribers are increasingly consuming music via playlists rather than via traditional albums. Music streaming has made international superstars of artists who may have not even have had careers if the conventional way of releasing and distributing music had prevailed.

The Digital Skills Challenge

Digital transformation is not about evolving or tweaking, it is a whole new mindset. The rules haven't just changed; there are no more rules. Acquiring, developing and retaining the right talent to drive this transformation is critical but in this ever-changing world just what is the right talent?

Not only is the demand for digital skills at an all-time high globally, but the very definition of digital skills is also broadening and changing significantly. Back in the late 1990s, digital skills effectively just meant programming. As the dot com revolution played out, strategy, design, project management and marketing became critical skills needed to help businesses thrive. By 2021 the skills companies need for the digital economy have broadened even further fuelling intense demand for talent with skills as diverse as product management, data science, solutions sales, customer service and recruiting. This demand for digital skills is being felt at every level all the way up to the boardroom. The trend for appointing CTOs has been usurped by the board level appointments of chief digital officers with much broader strategic remits to drive digital transformation through every aspect of the company's activity and structure. We are now at the stage where classifying what are and are not digital jobs is getting confusing. In the UK government-supported 2018 Tech Nation report into the UK digital economy, they use the following classifications:

- **Digital tech jobs:** includes all people working in digital tech occupations, irrespective of the industry. For example, a software developer working in a retail company.
- **Digital tech jobs in digital tech:** includes only people working in digital tech occupations in the digital tech industries. For example, a software developer working in a web development firm.
- **Jobs in digital tech:** includes all people working in digital tech industries, including non-digital jobs. For example, an accountant working in a web development firm.[13]

The report cites growth in employment in the UK digital tech sector of 13.2% between 2014 and 2017 and interestingly also indicates that workers in digital tech are more productive than those in non-digital sectors by an average of £10,000 per person per annum.

The COVID-19 pandemic has forced an even faster acceleration in the creation of digital jobs. In September 2021 job search engine

Adzuna reported that one in eight job opportunities in the UK were in the digital sector. This represents a 42% growth from pre-pandemic levels in 2019.[14] The logical conclusion is that every business will eventually be a digital business in some way. It follows then that most existing jobs and skills will be repurposed for our digital economy if they haven't been already. At the same time, a raft of new skills will be created to help companies drive the innovation they now need to survive and thrive.

The broadening range and the large number of digital jobs are exacerbating skills shortages that have been prevalent in the high-tech industries for decades. However, the potential economic damage of these skills shortages is unprecedented and has the potential to harm not just companies but the economy of entire countries. Research for the Korn Ferry Institute published in July 2018 illustrates the scale of the problem. They predict that by 2030 in the technology, media and telecommunications sectors alone there will be a global labour shortage of 4.3 million workers leading to an unrealized economic output of $449.7 billion globally.[15] It is also clear that the economic impact of skill shortages is already being felt around the globe. In the UK, research from the Open University estimates that the current skills gap is costing businesses £2.2 billion a year in higher salaries, recruitment costs and temporary staffing. They also reported that even by 2018, 91% of UK employers were struggling to recruit workers with the right skills.[16] In 2021 TechUK reported that there are now 100,000 unfilled vacancies per month in the UK and that the skills mismatch is costing the UK £6.3 billion in lost GDP. They also highlighted the lack of progress in fixing this problem:

'The UK does not yet have the infrastructure and resources it needs to meet this challenge. The provision of reskilling and retraining remains fragmented and sub-scale and business investment in reskilling remains very low, especially among SMEs, which are the biggest employer. This needs to change.' [17]

This is not just the case in the UK, it is a global problem. Many companies are not yet set up to provide education, learning and development to produce the skills that are required now and in the future. In their research report exploring the transformation of corporate learning, Accenture predicted that if inadequate corporate training systems were not improved by adopting radical learning approaches, then G20 countries could lose out on £8.8 trillion of GDP growth potential from the investment intelligent technologies.[18]

Education systems are also currently falling short in terms of delivering the future talent that is needed, and this is often despite efforts from governments to fix the problem. Based on the advice taken from employers, the UK government recently radically changed the way computing is taught in schools, scrapping the Information, Communication and Technology GCSE and replacing it with more useful computer science qualifications. However, despite an increasing number of schools offering the new GCSE and A-Level, take-up has been disappointing. The Roehampton Annual Computing Education report revealed that in 2018 only 11.9% of students were taking computer science at GCSE and 2.7% at A-Level.[19]

The diversity issue

It's not just skill shortages that are the issue. There is a shocking lack of diversity in the digital sector which not only harms the employers themselves; it also hurts the customers they are creating products and services for. CNBC editor Lori Ioannou writes that: 'Silicon Valley may be the world's leading hotbed of innovation and genius, but it struggles with diversity and unconscious bias.'[20] She identifies this as 'an Achilles' heel' that is adversely affecting the industry, 'because having a diverse workforce is a competitive advantage that drives productivity and profits as companies sell their products and services to a broad population.' The well-documented issues with diversity in the digital sector are by no means limited to Silicon Valley. The UK also has its own diversity issue. Tech Nation outlines that only 19% of the digital technology workforce is female which compares poorly against 49% across all UK jobs. Black, Asian and ethnic minority representation also falls short of representing the UK population.[21]

Transformational thinking

In summary, companies are facing an unprecedented challenge when it comes to the skills and talent they need to thrive in a world of digital transformation, and these unprecedented challenges are going to need some unique solutions to solve them. It is perhaps tempting to think that some of the solutions which helped prevent the millennium bug from doing its worst 20 years ago are the answer this time. Why can't businesses and governments just throw money at the problem to solve it? The millennium bug was caused by a single point of coding failure that was understood and had a non-negotiable deadline. Governments made interventions to ensure the continuity of daily life and businesses co-operated as they understood the importance of millennium bug compliance throughout their supply chains. Ultimately the problem was understood, well defined and easy to fix.

Digital transformation is tearing up the rule books and throwing money at existing methodologies, tools and techniques is not going to bring about the radical changes that are necessary. In order for businesses to effectively digitally transform, they need to also transform their thinking and approaches around talent, and we've written this book to help them do just that.

Digital transformation is forcing businesses to think differently. The employers who are successful at navigating this rapidly changing business landscape will be the ones who also think differently about talent. This book will examine what it means to think differently by exploring these key questions:

- How important is the role of talent in digital transformation?
- What are the skills that are needed?
- How do employers find, keep and develop the right talent for these changing times?

It is already very clear that transformational thinking is required; while there have been some changes in some places in the last few years fundamentally most employers are doing the same things they have done for decades. Issues such as inflexible attitudes to flexible working, outdated recruiting practice, the prevalence of annual reviews despite a consensus on their lack of effectiveness, command

and control leadership and toxic work cultures are hugely problematic. While we cannot offer all the solutions, we have scanned the industry looking for new thinking and emerging best practices in key areas of the digital talent economy.

Endnotes

1 Gresham College. What Really Happened in Y2K? (online video) 4 April 2017. www.gresham.ac.uk/lectures-and-events/what-really-happened-in-y2k (archived at https://perma.cc/7Z9W-5LAA)

2 Office of the Press Secretary, United States. Remarks By The President Concerning The Year 2000 Conversion, *Tech Law Journal*, 1998. www.techlawjournal.com/congress/y2k/80714clin.htm (archived at https://perma.cc/U8Y6-F2MS)

3 Computerworld. Y2K Quotes of Note, 1 January 2000. www.computerworld.com/article/2597263/y2k-quotes-of-note.html (archived at https://perma.cc/6MJV-X7LN)

4 Computerworld. Y2K Quotes of Note, 1 January 2000. www.computerworld.com/article/2597263/y2k-quotes-of-note.html (archived at https://perma.cc/7NCJ-XG5R)

5 CNN Money. India Leading Y2K Change, 17 March 1999. money.cnn.com/1999/03/17/technology/y2k_pkg/ (archived at https://perma.cc/JCJ5-HR8S)

6 Statista. Worldwide E-Commerce Share Of Retail Sales From 2015 to 2024, 7 July 2021. https://www.statista.com/statistics/534123/e-commerce-share-of-retail-sales-worldwide/ (archived at https://perma.cc/473Q-AXZK)

7 Kinsta. Mind-Blowing LinkedIn Statistics and Facts, 20 July 2021. kinsta.com/blog/linkedin-statistics/ (archived at https://perma.cc/563A-PZD8)

8 Statista. Number of monthly active Facebook users worldwide as of 3rd quarter 2021, 1 November 2021. www.statista.com/statistics/264810/number-of-monthly-active-facebook-users-worldwide/ (archived at https://perma.cc/4KS6-F9S6)

9 R Kats. Netflix Statistics: How Many Subscribers Does Netflix Have? Worldwide, US Member Count And Growth, Insider Intelligence, 30 July 2021. www.insiderintelligence.com/insights/netflix-subscribers/ (archived at https://perma.cc/PGV3-S27E)

10 Consultancy UK. Covid-19 has accelerated digital transformation by seven years, 14 December 2020.https://www.consultancy.uk/news/26372/covid-19-has-accelerated-digital-transformation-by-seven-years (archived at https://perma.cc/74U7-5RQ8)

11 Lloyd's Bank. UK Consumer Digital Index 2021, www.lloydsbank.com/assets/
media/pdfs/banking_with_us/whats-happening/210513-lloyds-consumer-
digital-index-2021-report.pdf (archived at https://perma.cc/8Q4J-V269)

12 T Goodwin (2018) *Digital Darwinism: Survival of the fittest in the age of
business disruption*, Kogan Page Inspire, New York, NY

13 Tech Nation Report 2018. technation.io/insights/report-2018 (archived at
https://perma.cc/CJ5W-HF6Q)

14 B Cotton. UK Tech Boom Sees One In Eight Job Opportunities In Digital
Sector, Business Leader, 27 September 2021. www.businessleader.co.uk/
uk-tech-boom-sees-one-in-eight-job-opportunities-in-digital-sector/ (archived
at https://perma.cc/88S8-GRP6)

15 Korn Ferry Institute. Future of Work: The Global Talent Crunch www.
kornferry.com/content/dam/kornferry/docs/pdfs/KF-Future-of-Work-Talent-
Crunch-Report.pdf (archived at https://perma.cc/MU9C-38FS)

16 OU News. Report. The UK skill shortage is costing organisations £6.3 billion
[blog] https://www.open.ac.uk/business/apprenticeships/blog/uk-skills-
shortage-costing-organisations-%C2%A363-billion (archived at https://perma.
cc/XL72-X4A8)

17 Tech UK. Fast Forward for Digital Jobs, www.techuk.org/shaping-policy/
fast-forward-for-digital-jobs-report.html (archived at https://perma.cc/
RDW5-EUMF)

18 Accenture. Future Workforce: It's Learning. Just Not As We Know It, 18
September 2018. www.accenture.com/gb-en/insights/future-workforce/
transforming-learning (archived at https://perma.cc/28K9-8WQG)

19 BCS. The Roehampton Annual Computing Education Report, www.bcs.org/
category/19331 (archived at https://perma.cc/3GLB-PSPX)

20 L Ioannou. Silicon Valley's Achilles' Heel Threatens To Topple Its Supremacy
In Innovation, CNBC, 20 June 2018. www.cnbc.com/2018/06/20/silicon-
valleys-diversity-problem-is-its-achilles-heel.html (archived at https://perma.
cc/7JA2-6DFK)

21 Tech Nation. How we measure jobs in the 2018 Tech Nation Report,
technation.io/insights/report-2018/jobs-and-skills/ (archived at https://perma.
cc/4YZC-6RHH)

01

Digital skills for a digital transformation

In their 2017 *Global Human Capital Trends* report,[1] Deloitte Consulting reported that 51% of the companies they researched were currently in the process of redesigning their organizations for digital business models. Their human capital leader, Erica Volini, wrote in the report that organizations looking to become digital need to 'start with defining what "digital" really means'. She noted that too many businesses use the term digital purely to mean the implementation of new technology, whereas she believed 'it's really the integration of technology with a shift in mindset'. Statistics like this have been common for a few years, and they continue to grow exponentially, particularly as firms have responded to the economic changes brought about by evolving consumer and employee preferences, as well as sudden events such as the COVID-19 pandemic. The figures may change, but the trend line has consistently shown a steady rise as more and more businesses have 'gone digital'. Those two words in themselves can be interpreted in different ways. For many, the growth in digital technology platforms has completely changed the way their business is transacted. As consumers, we do a lot online, and our expectations have risen. A business that doesn't offer a responsive, more intuitive website or mobile experience, that can make our selection and ordering faster and easier, will likely face falling revenues. For this reason, many businesses have tried to recreate their offering through online sites, without first looking at what it takes to be a 'digital business'.

The new businesses that have grown quickly to dominate their markets have not merely tried to redesign an existing offering through a different medium but have created a whole new business infrastructure designed to innovate, restructure, and consistently lead the way in consumer expectations. This requires an organizational structure, culture and attitude that is new and bold, constantly evolving, and able to respond immediately to the smallest shifts in expectations, all while innovating and incorporating every new development in technology.

During an interview with *Forbes* magazine[2] following the publication of the Deloitte report we quoted above, Erica Volini drew out the differences between the digitalization of company processes, and the need to have a completely different mindset – both at a corporate level and at an individual level – to think and act like a digital business. It is this mindset, which broadly blends cultural change at a corporate level with shifts in the skills, knowledge and thinking required at an individual employee level, that we will be exploring in this chapter as we start to look at what we mean by 'digital talent'. Erica explained during the interview that this new mindset 'requires organizations to rethink everything from how they are structured to what the concept of a "job" means in the digital world, and to how to evaluate and reward individuals.' An example of this is the traditional organizational hierarchical structure, which can become limiting. If the business needs to encourage more collaboration and networking, through open communication and agile workflows could a more rigid hierarchy and management structure facilitate this? In all likelihood, the answer is no.

Understanding and shaping the new ways of thinking that organizations will need to embrace if they are to truly be a digital business has been on the agenda of consultants and analysts for a few years. Consulting firms need to stay one step ahead of their clients to be able to advise and lead, so most of them have spent the last few years researching the various aspects of digital transformation and what it means for their clients. The need for a cultural shift, which underpins a move from a fixed mindset to a growth mindset within the employee base, is a fertile ground for consulting projects, so is a much researched topic. For example, when the leading global consulting firm Gartner launched their 'Digital Business Requires a New Mindset, Not Just New Technology' report,[3] their research analyst Aashish Gupta was quoted on their website[4] saying 'For any transformation to be successful, people need to buy into your vision. The culture aspect and the technology demand equal attention because culture will form the backbone of all change initiatives for their digital business transformation.'

As the quotes from Erica Volini at the start say, many businesses see digital change and transformation as being mainly about technology, and usually from the aspect of simplifying and streamlining the people processes. Inevitably this will also help with cost reductions, as technology takes over jobs such as processing, analysing, recording, validating and reporting, which historically have been performed by humans, and in some cases whole teams and departments. We will be exploring in more detail the tasks that have been digitized and automated, and the roles that humans are now best placed to perform, throughout the book.

The automation of simple HR processes can carry its own problems though, specifically for the employees. Those who have been with a business for a few years are usually comfortable with the way it operates. They understand the internal systems and rituals; the way work gets done and the way their contribution impacts on the greater corporate output and mission. Now start to automate some of the operational processes and see what happens. What is the effect of replacing simple tasks such as the reclaiming of expenses, booking leave or setting up a meeting, with something that is automated and digital? Starting with the former task, instead of manually completing an expenses form, attaching receipts and sending it to whoever manages the expense claims, they now probably have an automated system to follow. Each expense will have its own code and classification, as will the reason for incurring the expense. Receipts will have to be scanned onto the system and attached to the submission, which will be done through a portal or website. The claim then disappears 'into the ether' and the employee waits to log in and find their next (electronic) payslip to check they have been refunded. To the organization, this process is now simplified, helping greatly with accounting and reporting, cost allocation and management. It is streamlined and straightforward. To the employee, this is a change and not one they have sought. The way they do a small, incidental part of their role is now different. Initially, they are likely to see this new process as less simple, and more complex. Where is their gain? This might seem a small and relatively insignificant change to how an everyday action is completed. However, for employees, it is a change. It interrupts their flow and gets them to think differently. If they are already working for the company, then they will need to feel that this change benefits them and the way their job is done. If they are new to the business, with no previous experience of claiming expenses any other way, they will still need to feel that the process is intuitive and simple, not unlike the everyday transactions that they are more used to.

Crucially, when we interviewed three employees from the same company (a multinational business in the transportation sector) during our research, each representing a different age group and length of service record, about this small process change in their own organization, all felt their new system for claiming expenses to be clunky and difficult. All felt that the process had been complicated on purpose to make claiming expenses difficult, and therefore less likely to happen if the amount was small. Even the youngest worker we spoke to, in her mid-20s, felt this way. She said, 'I don't think they care if I know how to do it properly or not. It's better for them if I don't know, because then I can't reclaim expenses.' Not only had this change not made sense, but they also felt it had happened for negative reasons. In fact, the change had risked creating negative attitudes towards the organization, at a time when most are concerned about 'employee engagement'. This was borne out by Anne Helen Petersen, a senior journalist with *Buzzfeed News,* when writing for the site in January 2019 in her article 'How the Millennials Became The Burnout Generation'.[5] She said, 'Many of the tasks millennials find paralyzing are ones that are impossible to optimize for efficiency, either because they remain stubbornly analogue or because companies have optimized themselves, and their labour, so as to make the experience as arduous as possible for the user (anything to do with insurance, or bills, or filing a complaint)'. For many workers, both younger and older, the seamlessness of the digital experience they get in much of their personal lives isn't matched by the one they get from work. If we extrapolate the example of reclaiming expenses to a much bigger task, resulting in how major and detailed parts of their daily activities are changed, then this will be more significant to the employee and a possible cause for concern. What is the purpose of the change? Are they doing it correctly? What is happening with the information? What will happen to their job?

In their October 2018 research report on our relationship with technology in the workplace, global consultancy firm PWC[6] found that around half of employees (from a global sample of 12,000) prefer a primarily digital interface when completing HR administrative tasks. However, they quote an unnamed US sales executive, interviewed for the report, who says 'I enjoy what I'm doing, but it can become a grind when I have a transaction and I have to run through all these programs'. This is something we will no doubt return to in the book many times, that a digital transformation, be it a simple task or major process, is part of an organizational change. The way that someone does their job has changed and the questions will always be around whether we have supported them properly and brought them with us on the change to help them own what they now do, as much as the impact on the business. Is the change something that helps employees, or is it something that's done to them? Do they feel it makes their working life easier or more difficult, maybe on purpose? And how will that affect engagement and morale?

In his 2014 book *The Organized Mind*, the New York Times best-selling author and neuroscientist Daniel J. Levitin[7] writes of how one of the hopes for computerization (and digitization) was to relegate the repetitive drudgery of work to machines, allowing humans to pursue loftier purposes and to have more leisure time, but that this is not being achieved. He says, 'Instead of more time, most of us have less. Companies large and small have off-loaded work onto the backs of consumers. Things that used to be done for us, as part of the value-added service of working with a company, we are now expected to do ourselves' This is what the writer Craig Lambert refers to as 'shadow work'[8] in his 2015 book of that name – 'all the unpaid tasks we do on behalf of businesses and organizations. It has slipped into our routines stealthily'. This is hugely important. 2016 research[9] from Ultimate Software, a US-based technology company that offers a cloud-based human capital management solution for businesses, found 92% of employees saying that having the technology necessary to do their job in an efficient way affects their satisfaction at work. Nearly one out of three also said they would quit their job if the technology at work is outdated.

The PWC research quoted earlier found that while 90% of executives believe that their company pays attention to people's needs when introducing new technology, only 53% of their employees agreed. And in our own research of 14,000 European job seekers, conducted in 2018, we found 76% saying that having the latest technology was an important factor in helping them be successful at their job. The way we use technology to help, support and enable employees is key to hiring, developing and retaining them.

As we start to explore what makes a digital mindset, and how we take our employees with us on the journey to a digital transformation, we first need to explore – and bust a few myths and assumptions about – the one area that dominates most conversations and thinking around digitization. Namely, workplace demographics. Or as it is more commonly known as, generational differences.

Millennial myths and other generational assumptions

In her 2017 research paper 'The evidence-base for generational differences: where do we go from here?'[10] Cranfield School of Management's Dr Emma Parry (a professor of human resources management) concluded that 'Evidence suggests that work attitudes are changing over time; that these are continuous long-term trends, not step-changes between generations'. In an earlier research paper[11] David Costanza, from George Washington University, concluded that 'The pattern of results indicates that the relationships between generational membership and work-related outcomes are moderate to small, essentially zero in many cases'.

I'm sure we've all been at various business and conference presentations and workshops when at this point a chart would be produced showing dates of birth, perceived personality traits and values and levels of digital adoption, of everyone born in the last 80 years. You'll probably know the standard categories:

- Silent Generation (born 1928–1945);
- Baby Boomers (1945–1964);
- Generation X (1965–1980);
- Generation Y (used to be called millennials by many – 1981–1996);
- Millennials (or Generation Z/iGen if you called the previous age group millennials) 1997 onwards.

These dates are taken from Pew Research Centre, a US-based opinion polling organization, which describes itself as 'a nonpartisan fact tank that informs the public about the issues, attitudes and trends shaping America and the world' and is authoritative in this area of research. Their landmark 2010 research report on millennials[12] had a strong caveat. They acknowledged that while generational analysis and searching for unique and distinctive characteristics within different age ranges and dates of birth, played an important role in social science, it wasn't an exact science. Their key conclusion was 'We are mindful that there are as many differences in attitudes, values, behaviours, and lifestyles within a generation as there are between generations. But we believe this reality does not diminish the value of generational analysis; it merely adds to its richness and complexity'.

When discussing technology and digital change in the business environment, most of the conversations revolve around the last two generations – their expectations and preferences. This is unsurprising as according to the Pew Research just referenced, it is those two generations who rate 'technology use' as their most unique trait. Looking at older generations it is their work ethic, respect and values that they feel are their defining traits. It's not hard to see how workplace generalizations start to take hold!

Most column inches in print media, and gigabytes of digital media, are concerned with what businesses need to do in order to hire and retain the people beginning to enter the workforce now, and those who have done so over the last 15 to 20 years, and who now make up the largest group of employees in the workplace. They are the group who have known technology all their lives and had the internet since childhood, so are most likely to be technology aware and want the latest gadgets and systems. Many of the conclusions are fairly standard. They are restless, they feel no specific corporate loyalty (after having seen their parents' lifelong devotion to a specific business or industry end in redundancy during a recession or business cycle downturn), look for purpose and meaning in their employer and their work, and want to feel valued in the workplace. They also want to operate in a culture of constant learning and development.

If you read our previous book, *Exceptional Talent*, you'll know that we are sceptical about the impact of a date of birth on people's attitudes and approaches to, and their expectations from, the world of work. Many of the traits just listed could easily apply to older workers, and will no doubt also be relevant to those who are in the early stages of their education. Most research around work attitudes that is regularly presented in mainstream media, and in the more clickbait-seeking part of digital business media, is nothing more than the guesswork that mixes correlation with assumptive causation, usually in an attempt to either sell a product or consulting service or over-simplify a complex area. Whenever the connections between age and attitudes to work are studied in a more controlled, academic way, it is usually concluded that there is little or no relationship, as our quotes at the start of this section indicate.

In an interview with the American Management Association,[13] at the time her book *Retiring the Generation Gap: How Employees Young & Old Can Find Common Ground* was published in 2006, Jennifer J. Deal, a research scientist with the Centre for Creative Leadership (a US-based global provider of leadership development), talked about her seven years of research in this area. She was quite specific: 'Our research shows that when you hold the stereotypes up to the light, they don't cast much of a shadow. Everyone wants to be able to trust their supervisors, no one really likes change, we all like feedback, and the number of hours you put in at work depends more on your level in the organization than on your age.' Jennifer's asser-tion was that while different generations might see the world in different ways, the main reasons that cause a perceived generational conflict were what she called organizational clout – 'The so-called generation gap is, in large part, the result of miscommunication and misunderstanding, fueled by common insecurities and the desire for clout'. This is largely to do with respect. Older employees will often expect their opinions and views, backed by experience, to be given weight, while younger workers want to be heard and have their views listened to. They may have perspectives and insights to share, and suggestions for improvements, that more experienced colleagues may give little weight to based on their perceived greater knowledge and experience. Although Jennifer J. Deal's book is over 10 years old, its central message, that all employees – whatever their date of birth – share values and expectations, want trustworthy leaders and want to keep learning to ensure they can do their jobs well, seems to hold well today. As evidenced by the quote from Dr Emma Parry at the start of this section, which is taken from her 2017 research paper 'The Evidence Base for Generational Differences: Where Do We Go from Here?' most of the assumed differences are driven by gradually changing external factors in how we live and work, rather than a collective response from a particular age group looking to differenti-ate themselves from their elders.

Writing on the LinkedIn platform in 2017 Sean Lyons,[14] associate dean, research and graduate studies at the University of Guelph, Col-lege of Business and Economics, summarized his 15 years of research into generational attitudes to work by concluding that the case for generational differences not existing was based on five assumptions:

1 That generations are homogeneous groups whose members are virtually indistinguishable from each other.

2 That generations are clearly definable, objective categories into which we can place people purely on their date of birth.

3 Through ignoring the fact that society is changing, therefore under-playing external cultural and attitudinal shifts and seeing them as changing simply through ageing or gaining more experience.

4 These factors are changing everything between different generations.

5 That the general narrative we consume through print and digital content is based on strong, robust research.

He concluded that differences are probably subtler and more nuanced than most commentators suggest, and it is the reporting and analysis of them that probably overplays their significance.

Research also shows that the economic conditions when someone first enters the job market have a major impact on their progression. For example, in the UK a young graduate first seeking employment in 2011 would be likely to have more in common with those who entered the jobs market in 1981 or 1991, than those from 2001 – even though the latter are technically part of the same generation. This can manifest itself through lower pay, fewer good employment opportunities and reduced investment in learning and development, all of which happen during times of recession or economic downturn.

A US study from Hannes Schwandt (Northwestern University) and Till von Wachter (University of California, Los Angeles) in 2019[15] found that the initial difficulties encountered when entering the labour market during economic recessions led to much weaker earnings, employment opportunities and career advancement up to 10 to 15 years out for workers across race and education levels. They went on to find that these initial disadvantages also have a detrimental impact on lifetime outcomes around health and relationships. We also cannot ignore the impact of external factors. Certainly, those who are in their 20s now are maturing into a very different world from their older colleagues. Consider this: in February 2016 I sat on a conference panel that was discussing attitudes towards employee engagement. Among four experienced HR professionals and analysts, the organizers had included a millennial worker. During the introductions, he said 'if I join your company and I don't like the way you treat me, then I'll leave. I won't be leaving because I'm a millennial who is hardwired to change jobs every few months to try and get on. I'll be leaving because you're a bad company to work for!' This went down well with an audience of HR people. And the young man had a point. When I was at his level I also wanted to be listened to, treated with respect and given opportunities to show what I could do. But I was usually told to 'put up and shut up', which I did because I needed the job. A secure job and an employers' reference was instrumental to getting a decent bank account and a credit card. Plus, access to finance – for a car loan (driving around in your mother's car wasn't a great look) and to begin saving towards a mortgage deposit.

Today's labour market entrants do not necessarily have such concerns – they usually get bank accounts when they're born, credit cards on turning 16, most have little interest in buying a car and as for saving for a mortgage? We know from the almost daily news items about the affordability of property – or lack of – that this may be beyond their reach. In fact, the bank that most young workers need to impress is the Bank of Mum & Dad – the very people who have been telling them to stand up for themselves in the workplace! However, even this perspective is not without its biases. In the Anne Helen Petersen Buzzfeed thought-piece we quoted in the last section, she did warn that many of the behaviours attributed to millennials (and which I have just added to) are primarily the behaviours of a specific subset of mostly white, largely middle-class people born between 1981 and 1996. Though she did also add 'but even if you're a millennial who didn't grow up privileged, you've been impacted by the societal and cultural shifts that have shaped the generation'. There is also a growing body of research that identifies life stage as a key influence on attitudes. Someone from the millennial generation is likely to change their values, and hence their expectations and prefer-ences, once they settle in a relationship or marriage, begin to raise a family or own property. The restlessness and fluidity towards work tenure that so many commentators categorize as millennial traits, hence needing to be addressed by organizations, are likely to be less important to those whose life stage requires stability and the need to financially support others. So, date of birth isn't the main factor defining someone's attitude to work. It is a more complex mix of external influences – both personal and economic – circumstances and mindset. In the digital world, employees need a digital mindset, and this isn't governed by their birth certificate.

What are basic digital skills?

The National Literacy Trust[16] states: 'Literacy is the ability to read, write, speak and listen in a way that lets us communicate effectively and make sense of the world'. Our levels of literacy are essential to our wellbeing, helping individuals to express themselves, interact and connect. These skills are at the heart of every job application and hire and will usually dictate how someone is able to progress in their career. They underpin personal development and learning, economic growth, good health, self-esteem, social mobility and personal fulfilment. Without them, the world of work and the wider society can seem a harder and more inhospitable place. As we prepare for the fourth or even fifth decade in which technological development and advancement have increasingly dictated the way in which we live, consume, connect and work, our ability to cope with a new kind of literacy is becoming just as essential to human wellbeing. The narrative that these skills come easier to younger generations does nothing to help more experienced or older workers and retirees feel included. People with a lifetime of knowing how to communicate, and what sources of information to trust, must learn these basic skills all over again. The UK Government has finally recognized the imperative of digital skills, albeit maybe a bit late. In 2015 the Department for Education (DfE) launched a digital skills framework[17] which defined the skills adults need to participate in, and benefit from, the digital world. This was last updated in April 2019 through a consultation (coordinated by the Lloyds Banking Group) which was overseen by a mix of large multinational businesses – such as BT, Amazon, Accenture and Microsoft – joined by government and NGO departments. The aim was to inform training suppliers and those charities, employers and other government departments that support individuals, and to establish a baseline of skills that are typically needed by those who do not use digital technology, or who do so rarely and with limited functionality.

We shall use this framework to explore what we mean by digital skills. They listed five categories of essential digital skills:

- communicating;
- handling information and content;

- transacting;
- problem-solving;
- how to be safe and legal online.

Their framework also distinguishes between 'skills for life' and 'additional skills for work'. The implication is that the basic level of knowledge and capability necessary for day-to-day living is insufficient for the workplace. The government framework also informs the Lloyds Bank Consumer Digital Index, which involves a basic digital skills' survey of 9,000 people. The 2018 survey[18] found 8% of the UK population (about 4.3 million people) possess no basic digital skills at all. Perhaps more concerning was that 10% of those in full-time employment had no basic digital skills, and those who are unemployed are almost three times as likely to be without digital skills. This is particularly relevant as jobs requiring digital skills are being created twice as quickly as those that don't. Of those in the UK population who did have some digital skills, 60% (just over 30 million people) thought their skills had improved over the last year. Given the distinction between skills for life and work and the growth of new jobs requiring digital skills, it was interesting that when asked why they wanted to improve their skills the main reason (given by about one third) was to improve their productivity at work. Yet only 6% of this group said that they had received digital upskilling at work. We shall look at this more closely in later chapters as it clearly raises questions over whose responsibility it is to ensure a greater level of digital skills for work. The second most important reason (given by around one in four) was to improve their own personal online proficiency. Further research showed that having better connections with friends and family and being able to better organize their life, were the two main benefits that people saw of using the internet, although saving money and being able to find a job also featured strongly. When considering digital skills in terms of the workplace, we can't forget how important they are to everyday living. Do we owe our employees a duty to help them better navigate their personal lives as well as their working lives? We know that helping them positively with wellbeing – mental, physical and financial – can pay dividends with improved work performance and greater engagement, so we need to be mindful of digital exclusion, something that we will look at later in the chapter. Returning to the DfE framework, it is worth looking at the nine core basic digital skills they list:

1 Turning on a device.

2 Using the available controls on a device.

3 Making use of accessibility tools on a device to make it easier to use.

4 Interacting with the home screen on a device.

5 Understanding that the internet allows access to information and content and that it can be connected to through Wi-Fi.

6 Connecting a device to a safe and secure Wi-Fi network.

7 Connecting to the internet and opening a browser to find and use websites.

8 Understanding that passwords and personal information need to be kept safely as they have value to others.

9 Updating and changing passwords when prompted to do so.

As we bring more and more digital interfaces into the workplace, it is worth remembering that 10% of the workforce – and up to 30% of those who are unemployed – are not able to perform, or understand, those nine basic skills. From advertising a vacancy, through the application and onboarding stages, the hiring process is increasingly digitally focused and may exclude those who are not up to the basic skill level, which is a problem given the number of open vacancies that businesses struggle to fill. Moving on from basic skills, let's consider the five categories of essential digital skills that the DfE framework recommends are necessary for life and work, looking at potential workplace uses:

- Communicating – essential for collaboration, connection and sharing.

- Handling information and content – finding, managing and saving digital information.

- Transacting – administering and managing transactions, which would include HR-related requests for leave and expenses reclaiming.
- Problem-solving – using digital tools to help solve issues and improve productivity.
- Safety – following procedures and guidelines to remain safe and legal, and boost confidence online.

The overall spread of skills and achievements that qualify for the five essential categories for work covers quite a range. Many people who have a basic level of digital skills can do some of these tasks, but some might not be as confident as companies would like them to be. We looked at a basic transacting scenario in the first section (expenses reclaiming) and while the people we spoke to could complete the action, it felt to them like hard work. Ease of task in a work environment is about more than having the basic skills, it's also about how the process has been designed. It is noticeable that the fifth essential category covers online safety and security, and this remains a major concern for individuals when transacting in their personal lives. Research usually indicates that around 80% of UK citizens[19] have online security concerns, with 40% saying they are very concerned. Their main worries are usually that their identity might be stolen, they might lose money that they can't get back, or they have a fear of being monitored. As many as one in four people say that they know someone (usually a friend or family) whose personal details had been taken in the past.[20] Each organization must take the online safety of their employees seriously and should help them to operate safely in all their online interactions. These concerns can have a major impact on how successfully an employee embraces both transacting and handling information. If they feel confident then they will perform these tasks much better, which will benefit their employer.

For all organizations, there are three areas of the digital skills gap that need attention. In a later chapter, we will be examining some of the opportunities for greater diversity and inclusion that the hiring and development of digital talent may offer. However, as we look at the current level of digital skills within the workforce and population at large, it is noticeable that the three areas that need attention are closely related to diversity and inclusion. First, age. In the last section, we looked at some of the pitfalls of following too much of the general age and generation-related narrative that exists. However, in the context of the research that we have looked at in this section it was shown that everyone under the age of 35 in the UK has some level of basic digital skills, but for those over 65 around 30% have no basic digital skills. We now see a five-generation workforce, with people working beyond standard retirement age, so employers will need to encourage adoption by older workers in a positive, inclusive way. Second, there is a slight gender difference. A higher proportion of men have basic digital skills than women. Although this gap is not large, it does fluctuate – from 6% in 2015 to 9% in 2017 and currently 7%. Again, the organization should look to encourage greater adoption by both sexes in a positive way, to help them improve performance. The final gap is of greater concern but does offer an opportunity for business. For the first time, the Lloyds index looked at the digital skills of people who were registered disabled and found that they are four times more likely to be offline. The main reasons they gave were a lack of motivation and a lack of confidence. With talent in short supply, we have seen many initiatives taken by businesses to source hires from the pool of disabled people who are not often reached by standard recruitment approaches. By offering the opportunity to gain confidence and a basic grounding in digital skills they can create a more inclusive culture and attract people from an often-neglected talent pool.

Having good digital skills is important for our employees

It is important to try and understand how strong the digital skills are across our workforce, and to identify where there may be gaps and how we can help people to close them. It is crucial for their productivity and wellbeing at work, and for their wellbeing and contentment in their personal lives. And it also helps people to feel more confident when we install new technology at work which might require them to transact their business in different ways. One other area in which improved digital skills will help our employees is in boosting their confidence during times of uncertainty. The sudden shift to remote working that many experienced in March 2020, as the COVID-19 pandemic changed how and where we work, would have seen them try to fully embrace virtual communication – such as calls through Zoom, Skype or Microsoft Teams – for the first time. The need to start using collaborative tools to work constructively and profitably with their colleagues may well have helped improve productivity and given them greater confidence. It is the way in which we support them during these times that can increase their confidence in their digital abilities. The period following March 2020 didn't only see a sudden adoption of collaborative working techniques, it also meant that all our workplace technology – whether for recruitment, learning, performance management or HR administration – was being used remotely. We will be exploring how this impacted talent acquisition in Chapter 2, and talent management in Chapter 4. What we have seen since March 2020, amidst a proliferation of new tools and interfaces, is what many in the workplace technology sector refer to as accelerated digital transformation, with an urgent need to digitize all parts of the talent journey. With this in mind, we need to start exploring exactly what we mean by the term 'digital transformation', and the key role that HR plays in helping our businesses, and our workforces, to adapt.

How can HR stay relevant?

Is HR becoming irrelevant? No, I'm not suggesting you close the book now and pursue another career, but it is a question *The Economist* asked in a 2018 headline.[21] They were writing about the 2018 Global Leadership Forecast, a report by Development Dimensions International (DDI), The Conference Board and EY following research among 25,000 business leaders and 2,500 HR professionals.[22] The report's lead author, Evan Sinar (PhD, chief scientist and vice president at DDI), had said one of the big issues leading to the decline of HR's influence in the C-suite has been their struggle to keep up with digital transformation'. To better understand what led the report's authors to draw these conclusions it helps to look at how they categorized the HR function.

They outlined the three types of personas that they saw HR professionals adopting. First, there are the 'reactors'. Practitioners who fall into this category are those whose main concerns are ensuring compliance with policies and legalities while having some basic talent management in place. The second, and more progressive, persona they identified were 'partners'. Similar to the traditional business partnering model, these HR practitioners work more closely with managers across the business to achieve talent goals and close skill gaps. They are also more likely to be involved with performance, development, hiring and workforce planning. The third category was classed as 'anticipators'. This signifies HR people who use data and advanced analytics to provide senior management with people insights and help with planning the overall talent strategy that drives business goals and outcomes. These categories are hardly groundbreaking. In some way, they have all featured during numerous discussions in recent years over how HR professionals can be taken more seriously within organizations and gain the aspirational 'seat at the table'.

The move away from predominantly administrative duties to taking a more strategic role in helping the business achieve its commercial goals has long been described as the goal of modern HR; creating better workplaces that can help people develop and thrive. It's no surprise therefore that to be seen as truly strategic, the report's authors concluded that HR professionals need to be seen to act as anticipators. If rationale were needed, then we don't have to look any further than the top two challenges that CEOs said they face, which were, by some margin, developing the next generation of leaders and attracting and retaining top talent. Only 11% of business leaders surveyed in the report saw HR fulfilling the role of anticipator though, with almost half (48%) seeing them as partners and 41% as reactors. HR professionals saw themselves in much the same way, although slightly more positively. Around one in six believe they are anticipators and the overwhelming majority (62%) see themselves as partners. HR's very honest self-assessment for this report showed few positive signs when looking at helping with the development of future leaders. Over three-quarters (78%) admitted that their leadership career planning processes were at best only moderately effective (or worse), while 55% had no integration of leadership development processes and 48% do not use information from assessments. Unsurprisingly, almost a third said that the relationship between strategic business plans and their own plans to develop leaders was weak or non-existent. These findings were probably quite predictable, but to fully understand the quote from Evan Sinar we need to consider other areas of the report. In an attempt to gauge how HR leaders' roles were changing, they were asked which of their challenges were increasing the most. The biggest increases were for embracing new HR technology, using analytical skills and needing to become a trusted advisor to their senior team. Further research found HR leaders admitting to being much less effective than other senior leaders when it comes to operating in a highly digital environment, using data to guide business decisions and coping with high-speed change at work. In their own words, HR professionals seem much less prepared for a new digital era of work than other business areas.

As we begin to explore what we mean when we say digital transformation, it will become apparent that the role HR plays is crucial. The way our employees do their jobs, the relationship they have with the business, the impact on their productivity and engagement, how they interact with colleagues and managers, the way they are rewarded, and even the very nature of the terms under which they offer their time and labour, are all changing, shaped by digital technology and a completely different mindset around what our organizations do, and what our customers and clients expect. HR practitioners can't turn their backs on this. It goes to the very heart of their role and remit within an organization.

A new approach, not an enhancement of an existing process

On a recent episode of the *Recruiting Futures* podcast,[23] author Tom Goodwin was talking about his book *Digital Darwinism*[24] and said 'the book is about the changing world and the degree to which we need to get really enthusiastic about technology and really optimistic about the possibilities it creates, at the same time as realizing that a lot of the dynamics that have made us successful until now, are either not particularly helpful in the future, or are even detrimental to our future plans'. He further explained that his views of digital business are not that everything is now different, and the pace of change is accelerating so fast, that organizations need to change or die. Instead, it needs a more reflective approach, accepting that if their business were set up today then it would be in a very different way. So, it is not quite right for this moment, which means there needs to be a careful rethink as to how it can be transformed. He gave an example of a business who told him they needed to get everyone to go about their jobs in a radically different way, and try to change their culture, but meanwhile 'understand that our company has made great decisions and our leadership has been incredibly smart and we can be really proud of everything we've done at the same time'. This dynamic is interesting. By writing a book about how businesses are transforming digitally, we are not attempting to say that there was something wrong with the previous way of doing business, but that some companies are now embracing new ways of operating, which means that to remain competitive other organizations will have to adapt. Tom explained, 'I think that the really important sort of tension to get across, is don't be too proud to change and don't assume that blame is attached to this recognition that we need to pivot'. It is important to take this more thoughtful perspective. The general business, print, broadcast and digital media – not to mention the conference and expo circuit – are constantly full of hype with a range of exuberant thought leaders, consultants and tech gurus desperately selling the latest trends that will change business as we know it.

Case studies tend to be from large, well established international businesses that are usually from the consulting, financial services, fast-moving consumer goods (FMCG) and energy sectors. They often have large budgets and a knowledge-based workforce who can easily adapt. For most organizations though, these innovations and case studies are a far cry from their day-to-day business problems. Businesses have many challenges, externally around commercial and competitive pressures, and internally through engagement, retention, leadership and development. Too much of the narrative leads them to believe that they can solve these issues with a new piece of technology, whereas what they often need is a change in culture, structure and mindset. Having said that, we can't turn our backs on how business is changing. The expectations of our customers and clients, employees and collaborators, are changing. They expect to do things quickly and efficiently, have information at their fingertips as and when they need it, and be able to complete tasks and transactions immediately with minimum effort. These are the developments we need to think about more deeply when we address Tom's point about how our businesses might look if they were set up today.

In earlier sections, we started to look at how a digital transformation is an organizational change. The example of how the digitization of a relatively simple procedure such as reclaiming cash expenses turned it into something more complex and time-consuming, showed some of the negative impacts that can happen when we try to enhance an existing process rather than rethinking the way we approach it. The three people I met all had negative perceptions about the business and their motives for change. One felt the company was trying to increase their profit by getting employees to absorb small costs themselves, which breeds distrust. This creates a twofold challenge for the HR team. The first challenge is to help prepare the workforce for the organizational and operational changes that will, by necessity, happen as part of any digital transformation, particularly one that impacts the business output. And the second challenge is to change the way HR services are provided so as to align them with digitization. This second challenge leaves HR having to transform themselves as well as support the rest of this business through transformation. Becoming a digital business is not purely about using devices or machines to do the same thing you've always done, nor is it about using code or algorithms to make operational processes quicker. It is about changing the mindset; taking a different look at what, how and why we do things. Research from LeapGen, a consultancy run by global tech analyst Jason Averbook, found that 75% of HR functions in large and medium companies do not have a unified digital strategy.[25]

In his recent presentations, Jason has stressed that the four pillars of a digital HR strategy are mindset, people, process and technology. To successfully integrate such a strategy means firstly that there is a clear vision and strategy with which people are aligned and engaged. Processes can then be designed around the user (i.e., the employee) and should be clearly linked to a business outcome that they understand. The technology is then there to support people and the processes while managing and delivering the data necessary for decision making. To adopt this type of approach, the various processes and initiatives that HR has historically been involved with need to be redesigned to fit with a newly created digital capability. You can see how in our example of reclaiming expenses; this has not been redesigned but the physical actions have merely moved online and been shaped to provide better data for the business. The crucial part, the employee's experience, hasn't been considered, hence there has been no buy-in from workers to the new process, leaving them feeling negatively towards the rationale behind this digitization. As Brian Kropp, Group VP of consulting firm Gartner, said when launching their 2019 HR Executives Priorities[26] report: 'Employees want their 9–5 to look like their 5–9. And employees' 5–9 lives are full of seamless, effortless experiences, largely enabled by digital technologies'.

At this stage, it's important to stress that while digitization implies speed and seamless efficiency, the process of digitizing is anything but fast. The pace with which technology evolves and transforms – driving customer and employee expectations – might seem lightning-fast, especially when compared to a more traditional 'business as usual'. However, experience shows that most hastily conceived plans, and digital value propositions will fail. Similarly, many companies themselves may fail when trying to quickly adopt a more streamlined approach to digital operating processes. It takes time to overhaul an external customer service offering to create a successful digitally orientated one, and the story is similar for internal processes. Or, as the Massachusetts Institute of Technology put it in April 2018:[27] 'Digital demands entirely new approaches for imagining, designing, delivering and servicing value propositions. Consequently, organizational transformation cannot be speedy'.

From a system of record to a system of engagement

Mervyn's first job was as a trainee accountant and my first employers were a firm of accountants with around 250 staff. There were no computers. In fact, one of the tax partners once told me 'I keep hearing that one day all the tax returns will be done by computer. I hope I'm long gone before then. I cannot think of anything more depressing'. We did have an office manager, who in the modern workplace would probably have been called a facilities manager. He had other responsibilities though. He was also in charge of what he called the three Ps – personnel, payslips and petty cash. His personnel duties consisted mainly of sending out offer letters, getting employment contracts signed, collecting everyone's weekly timesheets and taking notes if one of the partners or senior managers wanted to notify a member of staff that either their performance, timekeeping or appearance was not acceptable and had to improve. His payslip responsibilities were to make sure everyone received theirs on a monthly basis. The part he seemed to enjoy the most was petty cash, routinely taking delight in scrutinizing the claim before him and notifying the member of staff (quite often someone junior) that he wasn't reimbursing in full as he thought the amount had been inflated. We were based in central London, and he seemed to have an encyclopedic knowledge of approximate taxi fares for each conceivable journey (cabbies didn't give out receipts then). And he never refunded a tip that you had given someone, saying: 'that was your choice, we don't have to reimburse it'. Forgive the nostalgia trip, but in those simple and less enlightened office times, this man's filing cabinets (he had a lot) were pretty much the firm's system of record for employees. The partners and managers were responsible for the accuracy of the work we did, but if they ever wanted to know anything more about one of their team – hours worked each week, sick days, leave taken, salary, previous office or performance misdemeanours or warnings – they would call the office manager.

Clearly, the modern workplace doesn't quite operate like this. A system of record can be simply defined as an information storage system that provides the authoritative data resource for the business, combining all the individual data or information generated by individual employees and business units. Within modern management information systems, all this data will be contained in multiple sources (systems and locations) so by bringing it all together in one system of record, the business has a single consistent, authoritative location for all the data it needs. These sources can be varied and in different formats. The more data we generate, the more complex the system of record will therefore become.

Mervyn's old employers probably had relatively straightforward concerns. Questions they needed answering from the system of record might include 'how much leave do they have left this year?' or 'can you check the amount of time they spent with client x last month?' or even 'have we had to question their timekeeping before?' A far cry from today when questions around performance, productivity and capability will be answered from a range of data that is constantly updating. There have been other changes, which are more important. For example, cloud technology enables a lot of information and data to be retained much more easily. And then there is the user experience. In my first job, I had no involvement with my file. Other people – be it the line manager, partner, supervisor or the office manager – created the data about me (to use a more current description) and I never had access to it. This has now changed. Employees today create most of their data and, crucially, have access to it. Modern enterprise HR technology needs employees to interact and use it. In fact, research study after research study shows that the number one consideration for any business looking to invest in enterprise HR software is the ease of user interface. Organizations are transitioning away from a top-down, HR-centric approach to people management, to something more agile, offering their people a single view of the 'employee lifecycle', with the ability to take control of their own development. This is known as a system of engagement. The easy interface – often based on the user experience of modern platforms such as Facebook, LinkedIn and Twitter – encourages use and helps the individual to take control. As Josh Bersin wrote in *Forbes* as far back as 2012:[28] 'Originally conceived as systems to help HR managers administer various people practices, now HR software is really designed to help employees and managers manage themselves'. A system of engagement will only work successfully though if employees and managers use it on a regular basis, hence also becoming what is often called a system of interaction. We are reliant on individuals updating information and accessing it, so the technology we implement needs to be simple to navigate and user friendly. We also need to think creatively about how we use it as there is little point in buying the latest technology and using its enhanced capabilities to do old school HR. Too many HR professionals do not seem to see technology as 'their thing' but as a box that needs to be ticked. As we discussed earlier in the chapter, HR leaders don't see themselves as being effective in a highly digital environment. Many HR teams digitize to do away with paper, yet they still end up with paper to support their data and decisions. This must change though. One key reason is that businesses, and most definitely our employees, now tend to be much more concerned with the present and the future, rather than the past. Key employee events such as performance management reviews have always been conducted by looking back at historical data. Similarly, when hiring, interviewers have been too concerned with what prospective candidates have done in the past. We have technology that allows for real-time measurement and analysis, so we need to ensure it is used that way and not merely to collate historical information.

The digital business world that we are writing about for this book is more future-focused. How can someone perform in the future? Which of their skills and capabilities will we need to help them develop? What skills might we, and they, need next year and for years ahead? If we say a candidate isn't right for our organization, do we really mean that they are not right, right now? A new HR approach, driven by technology and evidence (i.e. data and analytics) is being developed. Our employees no longer need hand-holding; they just want to know that information, and learning, is there when they need it, and they can access it at a time that suits them. For HR the days of self-service are being replaced by direct access. They still have the responsibility to create, design and structure processes and policies such as performance appraisal, salary scales, rewards and recognition, leadership development, learning cultures and organizational design. These should still reflect the specialisms and traditions of their business and engage employees. But now these processes need to drive a culture that helps people achieve their goals, and enables them to do better work, allowing the business to achieve its commercial goals.

A culture of engaging and meaningful work

There is a famous anecdote that is often used when trying to define purpose and meaning at work. From Mark Zuckerberg to the HR consultant who spoke at the last conference you attended; it always gets shared as the definition of how to inspire your employees. It is alleged to have happened in 1961 or 1962 and involved US President John F Kennedy. He was making a late-night visit to NASA, the US space agency, and was being given a guided tour of the facility as the US ramped up its efforts to take the lead in space exploration. It's alleged that while he was being shown around, he saw a janitor with a broom in his hand and asked him what his job was. The janitor is said to have replied 'my job is helping to put a man on the moon'. Several doubts concerning the veracity of this story have been raised over the years, but you can see why it is often used as a powerful example. The lowly janitor didn't see his job as purely being to clean the corridors but instead saw himself as playing his part in his organization's mission to land a crewed spacecraft on the moon. The perfect (some might say too perfect) way of illustrating an employee's commitment to the higher purpose of their employer, and the sense of belonging that they have to the organization and its mission. Both of these are usually seen to be integral to where digital talent chooses to work.

Earlier in the chapter, I shared a story comparing my first job with that of a millennial starting today, explaining the reason why I had needed to keep my head down and press on with whatever tasks I was assigned, but that more recent entrants into the labour force can look for work that engages them. How they are treated, the opportunities they are given, and a feeling of identification with the business and what it does, are all important to employee satisfaction. This leads many workplace commentators to conclude that, in order to attract the young digital talent a business needs, they must demonstrate a higher purpose, and offer work that is meaningful. Another expression that often crops up in the narratives around engagement at work, is passion. For our janitor at NASA, it could be said that he was passionate about the organization's mission, which is why he so identified with it. Within many of the modern workplaces that have been built by forward-thinking technology businesses (such as Google and Facebook), it is often said that employees work there because they are passionate about the business mission. Job advertisements often include phrases like 'share our passion' or 'we're looking for people with a passion for xxxx'. Yet this can often be misleading. In a *Financial Times* opinion piece from April 2019,[29] business writer Emma Jacobs said, 'Of all the management trends since the turn of the century, the exhortation to find passion through employment is one of the most delusional'. She also referenced Sherry Linkon (author of *The Half-Life of Deindustrialization: Working-Class Writing about Economic Restructuring*) who had pointed out that passion at work was a privilege, with most people prioritizing earning money over finding purpose. We think that it can be dangerous to over-simplify each individual's motivations and expectations from the workplace with a blanket finding.

As we explore the concept of digital talent throughout this book, it will become apparent that those with the most in-demand skills are in a position to pick and choose how and where they work. While financial rewards will always be an important factor, many of those with the best range of digital skills can command a good rate of pay from whichever company wants to hire them. But money isn't always the only thing people look for. It might have been the case for previous generations, when rewards and status may have kept some people working in roles they didn't enjoy, for managers they didn't respect, and in businesses whose products or methods they didn't always agree with. But for newer entrants to the workforce, this scenario is unlikely to appeal. They know that the level of engagement they feel with what they do and how they do it is not only related to financial rewards. Two people, one earning £130,000 a year and the other £30,000 a year, can be just as engaged as each other with their work and employer. It is likely to be purpose, meaning and the chance to do interesting work, rather than just the salary, that will keep them at the company. It will drive a desire to learn, develop and grow. Meaningful work has many positive side effects that can decisively impact an organization. A 2012 journal from academics at the Department of Psychology, Colorado State University,[30] listed several that had been drawn from a variety of research projects conducted on people who said their work was meaningful. These benefits included improved wellbeing, better psychological adjustment, more cohesive teamwork and greater engagement. They also shared a belief that their work was important and had a higher value. The ultimate benefit to the organization is a strong financial performance. The latter finding was corroborated by an academic research paper from 2016[31] that concluded 'firms with mid-level employees with strong beliefs in the purpose of their organization and the clarity in the path towards that purpose experience better performance'. The authors identified higher purpose at work coming from two sources – the camaraderie between workers and clarity from management. They found firms in the US that exhibit both 'have systematically higher future accounting and stock market performance'.

So, if meaningful work can improve financial performance at a corporate level, while also leading to greater health (physical and mental), wellbeing, cohesion and engagement for the employees, we need to look at how we can create it. In Chapter 3, we will be taking a closer look at the employee experience that a digital workforce will be looking for when they join an organization, so we shall look next at how corporate culture can create meaning and engagement. Unsurprisingly, it is the attitudes and values of leaders that play the most significant role.

How leaders help create a culture

When addressing the 2019 WorkHuman conference in Nashville,[32] US entrepreneur, and COO of global food-service business Focus

Brands, Kat Cole said that her approach to management was: 'My job isn't to make everyone happy but it's to make sure you can all do your best work and achieve our goal. I would be failing you if I didn't make it happen'. For leaders to create a culture where people can achieve their best, where they don't feel a fear of failure, and one where they feel supported and empowered, will take an approach that is a far cry from the traditional view of leadership as something more autocratic. Trust in the workforce is one of the most important factors. During the same conference session, Kat Cole also said: 'People closest to the action know the problem long before the leader. But they don't have the language or authority to make decisions. Listen to your people'. It is important that leaders move away from being the people who have all the answers and instead trust the judgement of those who are closest to customers and commercial systems. One of the reasons that a janitor can feel like they're helping to put an astronaut on the moon is that they don't just see themselves as a doorkeeper or cleaner, but as someone whose day-to-day actions play a part in helping the company achieve their overall goals.

We shall be fully exploring the concepts of leadership in the digital age in Chapter 5, however, suffice to say at this point that the way leaders live their corporate values, and the behaviours they exhibit and nurture in their employees sets the organizational culture and helps to create a place where people both want to work and feel they can achieve their best work. As we shall see in Chapters 3 and 4, both of these are key for attracting and retaining digital talent.

In our research of 14,000 European jobseekers, we found that the three key qualities they look for in their leaders are accountability, honesty and ambition, which are all very human traits. The qualities linked to a more autocratic style, such as decisiveness and inspiration, seemed much less important to job seekers, even if popular culture often connects these with success in business through programmes like The Apprentice, Dragons Den and Shark Tank (US).

Accountability is hard for a leader. The best-selling US business writer and TED speaker Brene Brown[33] is a good touchpoint on this. She says that accountability is a vulnerable process that takes courage and time. And that the opposite of accountability is to blame, which is faster. When looked at in that way, we can see why leaders and managers who find themselves under pressure can often default to blame, which has a negative impact on workplace culture. Vulnerability in leadership is an interesting concept. Brene Brown always says that there is no evidence that vulnerability is a weakness, and instead defines it as 'the courage to show up and be seen when you can't control the outcome'. Vulnerability in an organization is essential because without it there is no tolerance for failure, which leaves little room for innovation, experimentation and creativity. We shall see in later sections how important leadership itself, and the culture it helps to foster, are to a successful digital transformation. Suffice to say for now that a culture of blame is not one that will support a successful transformation.

New opportunities to innovate

Earlier in this chapter, we quoted author Tom Goodwin. One of his more well-known digital contributions was a tweet that surfaced in March 2015. It was taken from an article he wrote on digital transformation for the TechCrunch[34] site and read: 'Uber, the world's largest taxi company, owns no vehicles. Facebook, the world's most popular media owner, creates no content. Alibaba, the most valuable retailer, has no inventory. And Airbnb, the world's largest accommodation provider, owns no real estate. Something interesting is happening.' By now these words have probably been viewed millions of times. Not all emanating from Tom, who found many others in his space reposting those words as their own on tweets, blogs and status updates on Facebook and LinkedIn. It set in motion a debate on digital business that is still ongoing. On the face of it, his words are true. Yet they are only correct if we interpret them in the traditional sense of what we understand by the words business and commerce. Uber, Facebook, Airbnb and Alibaba are not traditional businesses but are platforms, in the case of the first three they are connecting individuals who are providing a service with those who want to use that service. As Tom's article explained, 'these are indescribably thin layers that sit on top of vast supply systems (where the costs are) and interface with a huge number of people (where the money is)'. On the face of it, this isn't new. Before Uber, I used local minicab services, which were all small businesses, usually owner-managed. None of those small businesses owned any of the cars I was driven in. They were owned by self-employed cab drivers who paid a weekly or monthly 'rent' to the company in return for being allocated fares. However, the big difference now is that instead of me contacting the company, who would then contact the driver, the Uber platform gives me direct contact with the driver. I know their details and ratings and have a picture of their car. As it is a geo-locational platform the driver knows exactly where I am and where I need to go. And their maps will let them know the quickest way to get me there. And there's more. Uber now also has a lot of data on me – and not only where I go and what times I go there. They know my regular destinations (probably the homes of my closest friends and family) the restaurants I like, the type of cuisine I favour, the hotels I stay in when I go to the cinema, and much more. That data can be analysed and monetized.

Digital transformation is overhauling the very concepts of business and organizational purpose, but it is a mistake to assume that this is all purely about technology. On an episode of the *Recruiting Futures* podcast[35] Sebastian Kolberg, VP Change Management for Digital Transformation at Bayer, was asked how to approach digital transformation. He said that you had to start with the end – in other words, the customer – and ascertain the problem the customer has that you need to try and solve. Then you can apply digital technology and new collaborative working methods to solve the problem in a new way, creating new solutions, rather than purely designing a technology solution to solve issues.

Several of the new digital businesses don't necessarily provide me with a service that I want, but with one that I didn't know I needed. To find out which service, application or interface will be most successful requires a lot of research, modelling, trial and error testing and often a leap of faith from investors. For a company to navigate this successfully, allowing their digital talent to thrive, they need a working environment that supports and enables these processes.

The new opportunities to innovate come from the people, organizational mindset and collaborative working, and not purely a piece of code or software. As research scientists Stephanie Woerner and Peter Weill say at the start of their book *What's Your Digital Business Model?* 'digital transformation isn't about technology – it's about change'. This provides a challenge for businesses: namely, how to truly innovate. If it is the people, and the working methods, that will bring about this change, then this is something that HR needs to fully grasp.

A model and culture for innovation

Stephanie Woerner and Peter Weill's book provides some interesting perspectives on how companies are transforming their business digitally. Their previous research work had identified four models for businesses looking to thrive in the digital age, with the biggest success driver for each being the customer experience:

- Supplier – a business selling services, such as insurance, through another enterprise.
- Omnichannel – a business that 'owns' the customer relationship so can offer a range of products (e.g., banks or high street retailers).
- Modular – a business that is constantly innovating and adapting to a wide range of ecosystems. These are essential 'plug and play' products, an example being PayPal.
- Ecosystem drivers – these are the companies that dominate a marketplace, through their range of offerings and customer services. An obvious example is Amazon.

We have given a snapshot here, but it is worth considering where your business would fit in, and the kind of cultural and organizational changes that might need to be made if the leaders wanted to restructure and reposition the business. This change wouldn't be purely down to re-allocating employee duties but taking a more holistic look at information and knowledge flows, and employee connection points. People who have been used to working in hierarchical teams might find themselves collaborating across teams and divisions with people they may not have interacted with before. We'll explore these working models more in Chapter 5.

For a business beginning to plan for a digital transformation, there are a number of key questions to be explored. First, what are the external digital opportunities and threats? For example, how can your service offerings be improved, and where might competitors be able to move into your sector or customer base? This should include a look at which of the business models listed above a new service might fit into, while also exploring those where they might be able to gain a digital competitive advantage.

Meanwhile the key questions, for the purposes of our book, will be around organizational capability. Does your organization have the skills, knowledge, rewards, employee base, learning approach and cohesion to reinvent, or significantly re-purpose, what the business does? And perhaps most crucially, does the organization have leaders who are capable of driving a successful transformation? We have already touched on the role of leaders earlier in this chapter and will further explore the area of digital leadership capability in Chapter 6. To enable all of this to happen, a business needs to foster an innovation culture. In Chapter 4 we will explore the employee experience that digital talent wants, and needs, in order to join a business and to be successful.

By this stage, it has probably become apparent that a no-blame culture, a commitment to real-time learning and growth mindsets and finding a way of rewarding individuals that can focus on inputs as well as successful outputs, will all be necessary.

HR's role in digital transformation

As we have seen, it can be hard to specifically define the term 'digital transformation'. It will mean different things to different organizations. The standard definitions are often around the use of digital technology to solve traditional problems but as we have seen, often the end result is the creation of new markets and services rather than merely solving old problems. Some use the term to imply a paperless approach, but that fails to recognize the huge differences that digital technology makes to the way we work, access information and communicate. New digital solutions enable new types of innovation and creativity, rather than simply enhancing and supporting traditional methods.

Earlier in this chapter, we saw how HR professionals are, by their own admission, uncomfortable operating in highly digital environments. Many see their role as either reactors or partners but not anticipators. As the chapter has unfolded, we've tried to show that a digital transformation is not just about technology. It is primarily about an organizational change that encompasses different mindsets, new ways of working and relies on a culture of innovation and experimentation.

These are all areas in which the HR professional should feel comfortable. In future chapters, we will be investigating more closely new approaches to the employee experience and talent management, and the role they play in supporting this culture of change. Both these areas are firmly within HR's remit, so successfully transforming them will play a key role in shaping the organizational culture. It will require a more strategic, data-led approach, something which is not always in HR's comfort zone. Yet help is at hand.

Research carried out by PWC in late 2018[36] on employees' relationship with workplace technology (something we will explore in more detail in Chapter 4) found that from a base of 12,000 employees, at least half preferred digital interactions for tasks such as updating personal information, reviewing (and enrolling in) benefits' schemes and scheduling leave. Only a quarter wanted a purely face-to-face interaction. When dealing with more personal matters – such as performance reviews, giving or receiving feedback, or getting help with a more complex issue – still around 30% were happy to have a primarily digital interface.

So, HR operations itself is ripe for digital transformation. When looking at the shift from systems of record to systems of engagement earlier in the chapter, we saw how the creation of a digital interface enables the HR team to collect the data and insights they need to effectively support employees in doing their best work.

Too often we talk about challenges for the HR team, but the topics we are writing about here provide a real opportunity to help create an environment in which the organization can adopt the right digital model and create the experiences that customers and clients want. Which leads to better financial results.

In our previous book, we described the new talent journey. How the attraction, hiring, development and retention of talent was evolving, primarily as technology began to enable the key touchpoints on the employee lifecycle – recruitment, onboarding, learning, performance management, career progression – to become more of a seamless journey and less of a series of procedures that HR performs on employees.

In this book we will gradually explore the new digital talent journey, which takes this on to the next level, creating the right framework and culture to support a digital transformation and an innovative organization. In later chapters, we will take a more in-depth look at the digital talent experience, how talent management is becoming more digital and the important roles that leadership and technology play in creating the journey.

But first, in our next chapter, we look at the early part of the new digital talent journey, and specifically how digital transformation is changing the way we attract, select and hire our digital talent.

Chapter summary

Digital transformation isn't about technology, it's about change, about taking a different look at what, how and why we do things. Are we changing the way people do their jobs? We need to support and enable them as we would through any organizational change, so we can take them on their digital journey. As explored in this chapter:

- Do we fully understand the level of digital skills and digital literacy within our workforce? If we are asking them to work in a different way, will they need up-skilling or re-skilling?

- Can our HR team be classed as anticipators? Can they use data and advanced analytics to provide senior management with the people insights necessary to help plan the overall talent strategy for the business? Are we future-focused enough to forecast the skills and capabilities we will need in the future?

- Understanding how creating a culture of purpose and meaningful work will help to drive higher engagement, improved performance and productivity, and greater wellbeing among our people.

- Shifting from systems of record to systems of engagement enables the HR team to collect the data and insights they need to effectively support employees in doing their best work.

- Does your organization have the skills, knowledge, rewards, employee base, learning approach and cohesion to reinvent, or significantly re-purpose, what the business does?

Endnotes

1 Deloitte. 2017 Global Human Capital Trends, 20 October 2020. www2. deloitte.com/us/en/insights/multimedia/videos/human-capital-trends.html (archived at https://perma.cc/ZJ2Y-R7FL)

2 V Lipman. Practical Tips to Help Companies Develop A Digital Mindset, *Forbes*, 19 July 2017 www.forbes.com/sites/victorlipman/2017/07/19/practical-tips-to-help-companies-develop-a-digital-mindset/ (archived at https://perma.cc/ SW55-A9JH)

3 E Golluscio, K Mann, A Gupta, A Leow. Digital Business Requires a New Mindset, Not Just New Technology, Gartner, 11 September 2017. www.gartner. com/en/documents/3798763/digital-business-requires-a-new-mindset-not-just-new-tec (archived at https://perma.cc/E2S4-EFXK)

4 Gartner. Digital Business Requires Growth Mindset and Not Just Technology, 26 February 2018. www.gartner.com/en/newsroom/press-releases/2018-02-26-gartner-says-digital-business-requires-growth-mindset-and-not-just-technology (archived at https://perma.cc/R3K8-4QCE)

5 A H Petersen. BuzzFeed News, 5 January 2019. www.buzzfeednews.com/article/annehelenpetersen/millennials-burnout-generation-debt-work (archived at https://perma.cc/R2N2-A64S)

6   PWC. Our status with tech at work: It's complicated, www.pwc.com/us/en/
    services/consulting/library/consumer-intelligence-series/tech-at-work.html
    (archived at https://perma.cc/2HKC-6AZ3)
7   D Levitin. www.daniellevitin.com/ (archived at https://perma.cc/8CSN-
    WCNT)
8   C Lambert. About Shadow Work, www.craiglambert.net/about-shadow-
    works/ (archived at https://perma.cc/GSJ6-X7D4)
9   Ultimate Software. New National Study Uncovers Notable Shift in Factors
    Influencing Employee Job Satisfaction, Engagement, 4 October 2016. www.
    ultimatesoftware.com/PR/Press-Release/New-National-Study-Uncovers-
    Notable-Shift-in-Factors-Influencing-Employee-Job-Satisfaction-Engagement
    (archived at https://perma.cc/PNB2-5XU7)
10 P J Urwin and E Parry. The evidence-base for generational differences: where do
    we go from here?, 2017. westminsterresearch.westminster.ac.uk/download/
    f9124d9430b69b3df89f8a631919e4a56795e04cde20a95d33139865d2b
    cba21/200052/Generations%20paper%20for%20WAR%20v4%20241116.pdf
    (archived at https://perma.cc/J3BY-QL7P)
11 D Costanza *et al*. Generational differences in work-related attitudes: A
    meta-analysis, *Journal of Business and Psychology*, 2012, 27(4), 375–394
    researchgate.net/publication/257584336_Generational_Differences_in_Work-
    Related_Attitudes_A_Meta-analysis (archived at https://perma.
    cc/4JD2-BYKM)
12 K Zickuhr. Generations, Pew Research, 16 December 2010. www.pewresearch.
    org/internet/2010/12/16/generations-2010/ (archived at https://perma.cc/
    MA39-ENHY)
13 American Management Association. The Myth of Generational Differences in
    the Workplace, 24 January 2019. amanet.org/articles/the-myth-of-
    generational-differences-in-the-workplace/ (archived at https://perma.
    cc/7P75-N625)
14 S Lyons. Workplace generations – identity not destiny. 30 January 2017.
    linkedin.com/pulse/workplace-generations-identity-destiny-sean-lyons
    (archived at https://perma.cc/EWY8-T3FJ)
15 D Gill. Anderson Review Entering the Job Market in Recession: The Prognosis
    Worsens, UCLA, 8 April 2020. anderson-review.ucla.edu/recession-graduate/
    (archived at https://perma.cc/X7UB-87TJ)
16 National Literacy Trust. What is literacy? literacytrust.org.uk/information/
    what-is-literacy/ (archived at https://perma.cc/8SJX-QXHP)
17 Department for Education. Essential digital skills framework, 12 September
    2018. www.gov.uk/government/publications/essential-digital-skills-framework
    (archived at https://perma.cc/Y9BL-9WCX)

18 Readkong. UK Consumer Digital Index 2018– Benchmarking the digital and financial capability of people in the UK. www.readkong.com/page/ uk-consumer-digital-index-2018-benchmarking-the-digital-and-1271635 (archived at https://perma.cc/PRB4-29ES)

19 ReadKong. UK Consumer Digital Index 2018 – Benchmarking the digital and financial capability of people in the UK. www.readkong.com/page/ uk-consumer-digital-index-2018-benchmarking-the-digital-and-1271635 (archived at https://perma.cc/PRB4-29ES)

20 ReadKong. UK Consumer Digital Index 2018 – Benchmarking the digital and financial capability of people in the UK. www.readkong.com/page/ uk-consumer-digital-index-2018-benchmarking-the-digital-and-1271635 (archived at https://perma.cc/PRB4-29ES)

21 T Williams. Is HR becoming irrelevant?, Economist Education. execed. economist.com/blog/industry-trends/hr-becoming-irrelevant (archived at https://perma.cc/7LW4-RLUN)

22 DDI Global Leadership Forecast 2018, www.ddiworld.com/DDI/media/ trend-research/glf2018/global-leadership-forecast-2018_ddi_tr.pdf?ext=.pdf (archived at https://perma.cc/MJ6J-W59B)

23 M Alder. Recruiting Future. Ep: 172 Talent For Digital Transformation (podcast), 6 March 2019. rfpodcast.com/2019/03/ep-172-talent-for-digital-transformation/ (archived at https://perma.cc/XKG8-CW5A)

24 T Goodwin (2018) *Digital Darwinism: Survival of the fittest in the age of business disruption*, Kogan Page Inspire, New York, NY

25 GlobeNewswire. Leapgen Achieves 63% Year Over Year Growth Through Global Expansion, Key Customer Wins, 30 July 2019, www.globenewswire. com/en/news-release/2019/07/30/1893635/0/en/Leapgen-Achieves-63-Year-Over-Year-Growth-Through-Global-Expansion-Key-Customer-Wins.html (archived at https://perma.cc/A8MG-ZH5S)

26 J Wiles. Gartner. Top 3 Priorities for HR in 2019, 12 December 2018. www. gartner.com/smarterwithgartner/top-3-priorities-for-hr-in-2019/ (archived at https://perma.cc/RE8Y-PNPG)

27 J Ross. Sloan Review Digital Is About Speed — But It Takes a Long Time, MIT, 5 April 2018. sloanreview.mit.edu/article/digital-is-about-speed-but-it-takes-a-long-time/amp (archived at https://perma.cc/5VPG-5PPV)

28 J Bersin. The Move from Systems of Record to Systems of Engagement, *Forbes*, 16 August 2012. www.forbes.com/sites/joshbersin/2012/08/16/ the-move-from-systems-of-record-to-systems-of-engagement/#2bd21d4e47f5 (archived at https://perma.cc/97KP-33GW)

29 *Financial Times*. No passion please, we are British, www.ft.com/ content/6aa98f00-669c-11e9-9adc-98bf1d35a056 (archived at https://perma. cc/6AK6-75L6)

30 M F Steger, B J Dik and R D Duffy. Measuring Meaningful Work: The Work and Meaning Inventory (WAMI), *Journal of Career Assessment* 20 (3), 2012. www.michaelfsteger.com/wp-content/uploads/2012/08/Steger-Dik-Duffy-JCA-in-press.pdf (archived at https://perma.cc/9Z3F-YJ9U)

31 SSRN. Corporate Purpose and Financial Performance, papers.ssrn.com/sol3/papers.cfm?abstract_id=2840005 (archived at https://perma.cc/CNE5-FDVD)

32 WorkHuman Live. www.workhumanlive.com/ (archived at https://perma.cc/PN9N-FHCZ)

33 B Brown. The Power of Vulnerability, TED, June 2010. www.ted.com/talks/brene_brown_on_vulnerability?language=en (archived at https://perma.cc/M7B2-XDJ6)

34 T Goodwin. The Battle Is For The Customer Interface, Tech Crunch, 3 March 2015. techcrunch.com/2015/03/03/in-the-age-of-disintermediation-the-battle-is-all-for-the-customer-interface/ (archived at https://perma.cc/9UMR-F6KS)

35 M Alder. Recruiting Future. Ep 179: Digital Talent At Bayer and Allianz, 12 April 2019. rfpodcast.com/2019/04/ep-179-digital-talent-at-bayer-and-allianz/ (archived at https://perma.cc/FX9F-6GAQ)

36 PWC. Our status with tech at work: It's complicated, www.pwc.com/us/en/services/consulting/library/consumer-intelligence-series/tech-at-work.html (archived at https://perma.cc/2HKC-6AZ3)

02

Talent acquisition

Having set the scene by examining the concept of digital transformation and HR's role within it, it is time to start our exploration into what we view as the most crucial aspect to the success of any digital transformation activity, the talent needed to deliver it. For several years now survey after survey has indicated that a majority of CEOs recognize that having the right talent is the most important business challenge they have to address. For example, in the C-Suite 2019 Challenge[1] survey published by The Conference Board in January 2019, CEOs across all regions were consistent in ranking attracting and retaining top talent as their number one internal challenge. Meanwhile, the 2019 edition of PWC's Annual Global CEO Survey[2] indicates that 'availability of key skills' is seen by CEOs as one of the top three biggest threats to the growth prospects of their organization. The same piece of research reports that 55% of CEOs felt they were not able to innovate effectively because of their current skills gap and 44% had missed growth targets for the same reason. Despite this, there is always a feeling among HR and recruiting professionals that talent-related activities do not get the profile or resources that they need inside businesses. From a digital transformation perspective, it is interesting to note that in the countless articles, whitepapers, books, conferences and other content dedicated to the topic very few, if any at all, even mention talent. This supports the idea that lip service is being paid to talent issues, but they are not getting the strategic attention needed to ensure that digital transformation programmes are a success. So why is this? In a recent *Recruiting*

Future podcast interview,[3] the founder of All We Have Is Now, Tom Goodwin, suggested that there are two reasons behind the dichotomy between words and action. First of all, visibility. He argues that we are now in an era where companies are announcing change initiatives as part of their corporate marketing to illustrate to the financial markets that they are on top of digital transformation:

> If you're a large retailer, the best way to show Wall Street that you get change, is to have a drone delivery service. It doesn't actually have to exist; you just need to announce your intentions, or to do something with data and facial recognition, or announce some sort of blockchain initiative. It always comes down to technology because technology is the most pure way to signal that you understand the future.[3]

In other words, investing in technology is far more visible than investing in people. The second reason Goodwin suggests is that driving actual change in business is extremely hard as you need to address not just recruitment or retention but the entire culture of the organization. At the same time, this kind of long-term internal initiative is not the kind of innovation that plays to the financial markets in the same way. Announcements about investments in training or news ways of recruiting are unlikely to push stock prices up even when talent is in short supply.

Charlene Li, the bestselling author, analyst and expert in corporate digital transformation provided more context on this during her recent appearance on the *Recruiting Future* podcast. She argues that for successful digital transformation companies need 'The strategy, the people and the culture to line up against each other'.[4] In her view companies are bad at the people and culture part of digital transformation as they put 'too much emphasis on the digital and not enough on the transformation part of digital transformation'. In other words, focusing on technology rather than the adaptation, transformation and adoption of people strategies needed to make the technology successful. Li also highlights another key issue that makes the talent aspect of digital transformation particularly challenging for organizations. A key area of digital transformation is doing business in a different way and potentially serving a different type of customer and that is likely to mean a different type of talent is needed. This means as Li says, that the type of people and the way they are recruited needs to change as well.

In our view, the situation is even more complicated. It is likely that organizations will actually need two different types of people and people strategies to be successful at digital transformation. Not only do they ultimately need digitally focused talent to make the reinvented business successful, but they also need the talent to drive the necessary change, adaptation and adoption within the organization during the transformation process. For many companies, these will be two different sets of people.

Ensuring the right talent is available at the right time for digital transformation is undoubtedly a complex process with multiple aspects to it. As we will see later in the book, leadership, talent management, internal mobility, development and the employee experience are all critical. It is inevitable though that for most organizations, talent acquisition will be the starting point of the process. In the rest of this chapter, we will explore the talent acquisition challenges that companies are facing when it comes to digital talent and the successful recruiting strategies that are being put in place to overcome them.

Thinking differently about talent

The acceleration of digital transformation means that many employers are hiring for roles they have never had to fill before against a backdrop of intense competition. Gartner Talent Neuron's recent research report 'Competing For Talent In A Digital Age'[5] identified that 39% of all open job roles posted by the S&P top 100 companies were focused on just 29 jobs roles and that 90% of those companies were recruiting for each one of those roles. According to Gartner: 'Companies across diverse industries and across the globe are converging on the same talent pools.'[6] They give a number of different examples to illustrate highlighting where 'new and old world' industries are competing for the same talent particularly when it comes to software engineers. These examples include insurance companies developing software to assess risk, manufacturers digitizing their processes, farm equipment companies building tractors with built-in AI and existing tech giants such as Google and Microsoft who are continually seeking to enhance their own capabilities. This picture is mirrored all over the world in companies of all sizes and illustrates the level of competition employers are now facing. As well as an unprecedented level of competition for talent Gartner highlights another issue companies face when they are hiring for roles with skills that are unfamiliar to their hiring managers; this is the increasing number of people needed to be involved in the recruiting process to ensure that the candidate has the necessary skills and experience for the organization and the risk of dramatically increasing time to hire.

As we discussed in Chapter 1 the definition of digital skills is ever-expanding. A decade ago, it would have just included coding and development skills, but it now encompasses a myriad of other areas including marketing, sales and product management. It also includes recruitment itself. Many organizations with in-house recruitment teams report difficulties in attracting recruiters with the skills and experience to recruit specialized digital talent effectively and this compounds the challenges we are seeing even further.

A combination of recruiter and line manager inexperience can be very damaging to talent acquisition. Lack of engagement, lack of knowledge on the detail of specific skills, inappropriate recruiting processes and assessment techniques that don't measure the right things are just some of the problems that companies can create for themselves. All of these issues not only prevent the recruitment of the necessary talent but they can also have an adverse effect on the employer brand as disgruntled candidates share their negative experiences among their peer group and with the wider world through social media.

One issue that is notorious in modern-day corporate recruitment is the quest to find what the wider recruiting community describes as 'purple squirrels'. These are potential candidates with skill and experience combinations that do not actually exist. This could result from wishful thinking on behalf of the hiring manager or a lack of knowledge of particular talent markets from the recruiters. There are many examples of disgruntled software engineers flagging up job descriptions on LinkedIn which ask for 10 years' experience in software languages and platforms that have only actually existed for a much shorter period of time!

On top of all of this there is also the issue of credentialism, something even experienced recruiters and hiring managers can suffer from when it comes to sourcing and attracting digital talent. Hung Lee, a well-known industry commentator and an ex-technology recruiter describes the problem in this way:

> Credentialism. AKA "she must be good because she worked at Google" syndrome. It's a problem in most highly skilled, in-demand job families, but in tech it is one of the most significant barriers to effective hiring that employers have to overcome. We all know it's important to 'hire the best', but we need to understand what IS the best or rather, what is the best for YOUR business before we do anything else.

There is danger in employers rushing to recruit software engineers without establishing what 'good' looks like for their organization. Hung points out that employers may 'end up focusing on brand names on CVs and ignoring a much larger group of candidates who may be equally or even more well suited but just don't have the name recognition on their CV'.

The credentialism that Hung refers to is a symptom of an unhelpful attitude in recruiting that is difficult for many employers to shake off. In our previous book *Exceptional Talent,* we discussed the emerging belief that past performance is not actually a true indicator of future potential, highlighting the work of companies like The Chemistry Group who are helping their clients prioritize behaviours, motivations and values as better predictors of future performance than hiring on current skills and past experience. In the years since *Exceptional Talent* was published in 2017, this idea has grown in its popularity particularly in the digital space where new types of roles are being created all the time and employers are constantly having to adapt and learn as the business world evolves. Past experience is no longer a reliable metric for recruiting in these areas, if indeed it ever was in the first place.

Chapter 6 will explore the dangers of making hiring decisions purely based on perceived culture fit, but hiring people based on shared values and their ability to learn new skills quickly is some-thing that employers should be considering. When asked about his company's talent acquisition strategy on the *Recruiting Future* podcast Craig Donaldson, the former CEO of Metro Bank had this to say: 'First and foremost I want to recruit people who fit the culture of the organization, people who will share our values and bring them to life as the organization grows.'[7] This is an attitude that is reflected in many organizations and is driving some new thinking in terms of the types of talent that companies are looking for. In an article published in FastCompany back in 2017, David Pachter, the CEO of technology company JumpCrew, talks about their strategy of hiring people with no relevant experience into their sales teams. This strat-egy came about after JumpCrew discovered that previous hires they had made with no experience were outperforming other employees with 10 to 15 years of relevant experience. Their process is also team-orientated and they hire salespeople in groups of 10 and train and build them into a team.

There are drawbacks to this approach, and it is not something that will work in every hiring scenario for digital talent. As Pachter himself points out, if a company's product has a 'super technical sale'[8] then enterprise software sales experience is going to be necessary. Likewise, if an employee needs to recruit someone with a PhD in data science it is going to be impossible to recruit someone with no data science experience and train them up, certainly within any kind of reasonable timescale. The key lesson here is the importance of questioning whether you need someone with that level of skill in the first place or whether you are just being guilty of qualification credentialism. Credentialism and hiring based on outdated metrics could be seen as conscious biases which are making it very hard for employers to recruit the people they need for their businesses. There is also a massive danger that comes from unconscious bias in the recruitment process and again we will be looking at this in more detail later in Chapter 6.

There is also a danger in terms of looking at culture fit either in isolation or as the single decision-making criteria. Digital transfor-mation needs a disruptive mindset and hiring on the basis of existing culture can lead to a stifling of innovation and a lack of diversity of thought. Unsurprisingly then, many technology companies talk about 'culture add' rather than culture fit as they expand their teams.

Embracing this kind of disruptive mindset is yet another challenge that employers face when developing talent acquisition strategies for digital transformation. For many organizations, only a total revolution in how they think about both talent acquisition and HR will solve the problem. As Tom Goodwin says:

> I think most recruitment is based on the principles of risk avoidance and plausible deniability. We look for aspects like previous experience, degrees and all these very defendable and robust boxes that we tick. And I think for a while that's been okay, because we knew that the type of talent that we needed was found within the logic of following these processes.

He also illustrates how challenging things are going to be for talent acquisition teams moving forward:

> Now the talent we need the most doesn't fit into these categories... I think our future and our success depends on people who are actually quite odd, have and who might have strange ways of thinking. Darwinism was based on mutations and errors and oddities being essential for the progress of species, and I think as an industry, recruitment tends to be based on removing the probability of anything strange, or mutations happening. And that's a fundamental problem.[9]

Although changing the status quo in recruiting is going to be challenging there are some structures and processes that can be put around the concept of this kind of disruptive hiring. In her book *Rebel Talent*[10] Harvard Business School professor and best-selling author Francesca Gino argues that disruptive thinkers are fully engaged with their jobs and offer the degree of creativity to businesses that they need to transform. Gino identifies the five main characteristics that people she would class as 'rebel talent' have. These are novelty, curiosity, perspective, diversity and authenticity. She also suggests that if companies want to hire rebel talent these are the characteristics they should be assessed against during the recruitment process.

In the midst of this perfect storm of challenges, it is unsurprising that we are seeing a growing number of talent acquisition teams seeking to innovate their processes and methodologies to gain a competitive advantage in their quest for digital talent. Against this backdrop, we are seeing an unprecedented level of investment in the development of new recruiting technologies and the market is flooded with products promising that they are the silver bullet that solves all talent acquisition problems. We will look more deeply at the trends shaping emerging recruiting technologies in Chapter 7. For the rest of this chapter, we will explore some of the key elements of talent acquisition and look at how companies are changing and adapting their strategies to successfully win the battle for digital talent.

Talent intelligence

The first step in effective talent acquisition is understanding the availability and access your organization has to the talent that it needs. One of the key characteristics of the digital revolution that we are living through is the explosion in the amount of data available to inform decisions with every aspect of our lives seeming to be quantifiable in some way. While talent and recruiting data are at an earlier stage in their development than other more mature industries there is a significant competitive advantage to be had for the employers who are early adopters here. One such employer is Phillips. Phillips is a company that has undergone a profound digital transformation, moving away from some of its legacy markets and focusing heavily on the emerging world of digitally enabled healthcare solutions. This has driven the need for a profound change in the way they acquire talent as they are having to move away from attracting talent from their traditional competitors. Their Global Head of Talent Alan Agnew highlighted the fact they are now looking for new talent profiles from unfamiliar industries.[11] Phillips' strategic response to this challenge is to become one of the first employers to build a dedicated 'talent intelligence' resource. Their talent intelligence team proactively sources and analyses data which allows them to make informed decisions as they develop their talent acquisition strategy. The analysis looks in detail at specific markets to identify the level of availability of skills that Phillips need. The influence of talent intelligence at Phillips is profound and goes way beyond day-to-day recruiting and its analysis has influenced decisions around mergers and acquisitions and office locations.

While this is impressive, many employers might feel that they lack the budget and resources to build a dedicated talent intelligence team. However, with access to data becoming easier and instant analysis being offered by services such as Horsefly and LinkedIn's Talent Insights, talent intelligence should now be a part of the workflow of every talent acquisition team.

Understanding the audience

Recruiting in areas of skill shortage requires a huge amount of influence to cut through the noise. We will see later the role that branding and marketing play in this, however, it is impossible to establish influence without first having a deep understanding of the audience you are trying to influence. If understanding the availability of talent is the first step in the process the second has to be understanding the motivations and needs of the talent themselves.

We talked earlier about companies self-sabotaging their recruiting efforts via credentialism, however, this is just one of the myths that need busting when it comes to effectively acquiring digital talent. To recruit effectively in this area, it is important to break through the hype and focus on the facts. Here are three of the most popular tech recruiting myths.

Engineers are all introverts with no social skills.

We will see in Chapter 7 why this is not only not true but how it came about and how it has affected technology hiring ever since. Mass generalizations like this are surprisingly widely believed but not at all helpful. Debunking this kind of stereotype is important if you want to offer the right quality of communication within the recruitment process and the right working environment for people to thrive at work.

Digital professionals do not respond to emails or networking requests.

Recent research that formed part of Stack Overflow's Developer Hiring Landscape Survey[12] illustrates that 'traditional' methods of communication are far from dead: 63% of the developers surveyed indicated that their preferred method of communication was via email to a personal email address. Only 11% wanted to receive recruitment messages via a job site and as few as 4% wanted to be contacted via social media but this likely reflects the sheer volume of untargeted spam messages developers get from recruiters on these channels. The key to effective outreach lies in understanding the difference between spam style mass mailings, which are universally hated, and targeted, well thought out personalized communication. To deliberately subvert Marshall McLuhan's famous quote[13] about media, in this case, it is the message, not the medium that is most important.

Everyone wants to work at Google.

This is another aspect of credentialism and a very common mantra, particularly for traditional businesses that don't feel they offer the kind of cool, cutting-edge culture that they perceive that some digital businesses do. However, when you look at actual motivations it is clear that this is not an accurate representation of reality. There is a strong misconception that employers need to portray a certain image to attract digital talent. The right culture is certainly very important, but this doesn't always mean having a slideshow in reception or offering unlimited holidays.

The Stack Overflow research[14] indicates that the three most important things software developers are looking for in a role are compensation, the technologies they will be working with and the amount of professional development available. The opportunity to do interesting and challenging work is also a key persuasion point and it is important that companies communicate this effectively. There are distinct advantages here for traditional established companies. A larger more mature business can offer a level of stability and a size of client base that many start-ups and other early-stage tech businesses cannot, and it is important that they understand and communicate these advantages effectively. The marketplace for digital talent is a very noisy one and even getting the attention of your target audience is a challenge. Despite this, there are huge opportunities. Most of the marketplace noise is just that, noise. Employers can differentiate themselves by being the signal in this noise. To do this it is vital to separate the myths from reality and make sure you understand the reality of the right talent for your business and the best ways of communicating with them. Profiling and persona creation are just a couple of examples of the tools that can be used to make sure you are answering the key questions of: who we are looking for, where can we target them and most critically, why would they want to join us.

Employer brand

It's not just the marketplace for digital talent that has a noise problem. We are living in an age of unprecedented digital noise and distraction. Human attention spans have been shortening for many years now, and a number of studies indicate that the root cause is an increase in external stimuli in the last decade. A 2019 study by researchers at the Technical University of Denmark[15] reported that human attention spans have been shortening in relation to the volume of information available. It is clear that the incredible rise of mobile devices and the proliferation of social media are likely to be key drivers accelerating this. The added implications for talent acquisition are significant. So not only are there limited talent pools to target, those people within them have significantly less attention to give you. Even if your employer brand and recruitment marketing can get the attention of your target audience, keeping that attention long enough to get a recruitment message across is a challenge in itself.

The concept of employer branding has been with us for decades, but it has never been quite as crucial as it is right now. In today's hyper-competitive talent market, more employers than ever before are investing in their employer branding activities in a bid to convince their target markets that they are the employer of choice.

In his 2016 book *Pre-suasion*[16] psychological and marketing professor, Robert Cialdini identifies just how difficult persuasion and influence are in our distracting times. He suggests that the way around this problem is to start to influence people before they notice they are being influenced. This concept of pre-suasion is exactly what the employer brand needs to achieve. Employers need to create positive associations with their employer brand within their target audience long before they ask them to apply for a job. The aim is to build enough positive recognition to keep the audience's attention when it is most needed.

It is also important to remember that branding is essentially about differentiation. Most employer branding initiatives tend to be very internally focused, even if that isn't the original intention. As a result, one of the critical issues with the current state of employer branding is that many companies, especially those in the same sectors, push out very similar messages. A quick survey of the careers website of five of the world's largest technology companies reveals the use of very similar tag lines, giving the impression that there is nothing that really differentiates their employer value propositions (EVP). The old one-size-fits all approach to employer branding is also no longer effective. Large traditional businesses have a huge variety of recruitment needs and will be communicating simultaneously with a number of different audiences. The businesses that are most successful at recruiting digital talent have carefully curated a separate digital employment brand to break down any unhelpful perceptions and properly sell themselves.

The companies that are really standing out in today's market are the ones who are thinking differently about their whole employer branding strategy. Over the last few years, we have seen the concept of 'talent branding' becoming more and more popular. The idea here is that the best people to tell the story of a company's employee brand are the employees themselves, and this manifests itself both in initiatives that are under the employer's control and those that aren't. An example of an employer-led initiative here would be the creation of a talent brand hashtag to curate employee stories and experiences across social media. Employers such as Google (#lifeatgoogle) and Indeed (#insideindeed) have clear strategies in place which identify internal influencers and encourage content creation. Other employers have gone as far as using specialist employee advocacy technology to manage this process. One example of such an employer would be the John Lewis Partnership who are using employee advocacy tool Qubist to amplify the voices of their employees.[17] The key aim for employee advocacy in employer branding is to provide content that is transparent, trustworthy and personal. In practice, this means that employees are encouraged to share employer brand content and stories within their own social media networks. Technology helps this process and uses nurturing and gamification to encourage and reward the employees taking part. In the case of the John Lewis Partnership, this initiative is supported from the very top of the organization. The John Lewis Partnership are in a hyper-competitive market and see their own staff as their best asset to make them stand out from the digital competitors they are up against for both customers and digital talent as their business continues to transform.

In the feedback-driven society we now live in, it is now impossible for employers to stay in control of their employer brand message. Sites like Glassdoor and its growing band of competitors are becoming ever more influential in the talent acquisition process, offering anonymous feedback designed to create transparency around the employee experience. This transparency is something all employers should embrace and encourage because ultimately it is no good getting the right talent through the door if people then end up leaving quickly because the employer brand was inauthentic, and the employee experience was not as solid.

Business storytelling

One of the most effective employer brand trends we are currently seeing is the use of strategic business storytelling. The *New Yorker* journalist and *New York Times* best-selling author Shane Snow underlined the importance of business storytelling during a recent interview on the *Recruiting Future* podcast when he said: 'Great stories build relationships, and they make people care'.[18] It is not enough to encourage your employees to tell their stories and to be transparent about the employee experience. The employees who are really standing out are the ones who have crafted a storytelling strategy designed to bring their employer brand to life by appealing emotionally to their target audiences. This is easier said than done, and storytelling will be a key challenge in employer branding over the coming months and years. There are methodologies and techniques that can help the process though. For example, Shane Snow identifies four critical elements of compelling business storytelling. He says that stories should have:

- Relatability – be recognizable by the target audience and easy to empathize with.
- Novelty – contain something that has not been seen before.
- Fluency – be easy for the audience to understand.
- Tension – exploiting the gap between what is and what could be to keep the audience's attention and land the message.

It's also important to point out here that the format of storytelling is not limited to text. Pictures, videos and increasingly time-limited short-form stories via social media are all tools companies need to have in their employer branding toolbox. The key advice here, and arguable one of the most important things a company can do to attract and ultimately retain digital talent, is to invest properly in employer branding. The companies with the strongest brands will definitely be those with a competitive talent advantage in the future and that know that to stand out from the crowd is crucial. Developing effective content marketing and storytelling strategies will be critical to successful talent acquisition in the future, so getting a head start now is a genuine opportunity to beat the competition.

Building long-term relationships

Despite some recruiting software vendors' claims, there are no silver bullets to finding and attracting digital talent. There are certainly technology and tools which can help the process, but effective digital talent attraction relies on relationship building at a human level. If we were writing this book a few years ago the main focus of any discussion around talent attraction would have been sourcing. For many years forward-thinking employers have gained a competitive talent advantage by making sure they were able to identify talent ahead of their competitors. The desire to find hidden talent was the force behind the growth in the discipline of 'sourcing', which relies on the skills and cunning of specialist recruiters, known as sourcers, to use the internet to identify potential hires. Sourcing is still important but advances in technology are starting to automate the process and effectively remove any potential for competitive advantage. Finding people is still important but the key to attracting digital talent now and for the foreseeable future is all about building trust. As we have seen previously in this chapter, employer branding is absolutely key here but, at the same time, the power of targeted outreach and building long-term relationships are also equally important parts of the equation.

The most successful examples of attracting digital talent via outreach and relationship building starts long before there is a live vacancy. Jordon Meyer, the founder of Milwaukee-based digital marketing agency Granular, has successfully attracted highly experienced digital marketing specialists to his business without using job boards or recruiters in the face of competition from some very well-known employers in the same geographical area. As Meyer said recently on the *Recruiting Future* podcast: 'We have a lot of soft meetings that aren't really interviews before the interview. It's important to build a bench of potential talent'.[19] Meyer also underlines the importance of quality of interaction and the importance of using hiring managers for outreach or at the very least recruiters with a deep knowledge of the market they are recruiting in. Ironically, sourcing digital talent is made harder as a growing number of digital professionals are hiding their details from recruiters and sources online because of previous poor-quality interactions with recruiters. Performing this kind of individual outreach and 'pre-suasion' may seem easier for a small employer like Granular, with a handful of hires a year, than it is for a bigger employer to do the same thing on a larger scale. However, there are a number of large employers who are achieving the same kind of results. Some of this is facilitated by large high touch recruitment teams but continually expanding the talent acquisition team is not really a sustainable long-term strategy. More innovative approaches are desperately needed, and it is interesting to see some of the new techniques that are now emerging.

One example of such an approach to outreach and 'persuasion' is the 'inbound recruiting'. The aim of inbound recruiting is to provide valuable content aimed at specific target audiences to raise awareness, move them into a recruitment marketing funnel and then continue to provide great content and it gives the potential hires a great experience at the same time. Inbound recruiting is the strategy being pioneered by digital marketing software provider HubSpot.[20] HubSpot is expanding rapidly and have an ever-growing need to recruit digital sales, marketing and engineering talent in several locations around the globe. Their business is based around the concept of inbound marketing, and they have used their expertise in this area to pioneer the concept of inbound recruiting. HubSpot uses a combination of blogs, videos and social media and source content directly from the teams in the business for which they are hiring. This ensures authenticity and also creates empathy with their target audiences. Being acutely aware of the competitive nature of the talent markets they operate in, HubSpot uses this content-centric approach to move people through their recruitment process. They constantly analyse where people are getting stuck or dropping out of the process because they are 'having trouble understanding the HubSpot story'[21] and produce and deliver content to address these issues as they come up.

Whichever tactics employers use, a strategy of continuous proactive outreach and relationship building is clearly what is required for a competitive advantage in digital talent markets. As Hung Lee says: 'Employers need to commit to the community they want to hire from. The most successful companies see their role as not just "employers of people" but as ecosystem support for the community'.

In terms of how this could be done, Hung suggests that it might take the form of hosting an event or providing resources or tools for the community. He also highlights the importance of a long-term approach: 'In essence, it means committing to interact with people who might not be "hire ready" and persisting in doing so until they are or might be.

And continuing to do so even if they never will be'. He also highlights the challenge this change approach poses for many employers, 'Making this happen is going to take a major shift in the expectations and resources we currently have in talent acquisition teams'.

Workforce planning

There is also another huge challenge to consider. Proactive long term relationship building is not possible without an essential element of workforce planning. The most effective in-house recruiters understand the digital growth trajectory of their company and work to pipeline and build relationships with the right talent in advance of specific vacancies coming up. One example of this kind of strategic thinking is happening within the talent acquisition team at the technology company Elasticsearch.[22] With a very strong employer brand that resonates with their target audience, Elasticsearch has a strong inbound flow of candidates. However, to make sure they are getting the very best people and providing an effective candidate experience they have moved from reactive recruiting to a strategy-driven approach. This involves using data to engage with hiring managers to anticipate future demand and building a structured process that empowers recruiters to make decisions and minimise the kind of process delays that lose many employers their best candidates. It is fair to say though that currently, this kind of approach is not as widespread as it should be. In a recent member survey by the Forum For In House Recruitment Managers in the UK[23] most respondents reported that their company's approach to workforce planning and strategic resource demand was still 'evolving' and one in ten reported that their companies were doing nothing in this area.

The evolution of recruitment marketing

We have seen then just how important proactive outreach is when attracting digital talent. More conventional recruitment marketing is still of critical importance though in order to raise awareness by communicating employer brands, to build trust and persuade as potential hires move through the funnel and, of course, to target active job seekers to fill urgent roles.

There is always a focus on recruitment marketing during times of acute skill shortages but the modern-day phenomenon of reduced attention spans makes having an effective strategy more vital than ever. In recent years things have moved on exponentially from the days of putting job advertisements in the classified sections of newspapers and magazines. Job boards have matured and lost some of their early effectiveness; social media marketing promises much. We are also seeing an increase in the use of programmatic advertising in recruitment marketing. Programmatic advertising works by using technology to automate the planning and buying of digital advertising and introduces an exciting opportunity for more precise targeting and increased ROI. Data-driven marketing is finally entering the recruitment space, and it offers the level of sophistication needed to connect with target audiences beyond the reach of traditional recruitment marketing. For recruitment marketing to be effective it is vital that employers understand what data they have, where the gaps are and how to measure metrics in a way that is meaningful to talent acquisition objectives. Data-driven strategies are on the rise, but as things stand, many organizations don't understand what data to collect and how to measure them. This is where critical competitive advantage could be lost.

As the options have increased though so has the level of complexity, and many talent acquisition teams are left wondering about the most effective way to deploy their marketing budgets. In our book *Exceptional Talent,* we outlined a model that helps to simplify the landscape and make strategies more effective. By understanding and following these principles employers will be able to build an effective strategy, regardless of how complicated the techniques and technologies themselves become.

There are four elements to this model:

- **Attention:** How do you find and get the attention of your target audience? This is a step that many employers miss because they take this attention for granted. This would be an error in any talent market but when it comes to digital talent it can completely derail talent attraction.

- **Persuasion:** We have talked about pre-suasion in the context of employer branding and relationship building but it is important to recognize that when it comes to the recruitment process itself everything is fundamentally about persuasion. Unfortunately, many companies are failing to be persuasive with their recruitment marketing. Selling the opportunity and the employer brand is critical, and it needs to happen across all recruitment marketing channels.

- **Conversion:** With attention so hard to come by, converting any interest generated into an application or registration is absolutely critical. The standard of conversion in recruitment marketing is very poor, mainly because of the combination of the outdated applicant tracking system and ineffective careers websites.

- **Experience:** Almost all talent acquisition professionals would agree that providing a good candidate experience is critical. It is essential to acknowledge that candidate experience starts at the very first touchpoint a potential candidate has with an employer's recruitment marketing activity. Experience is something we will be looking at in detail in the next chapter.

Chapter summary

Talent acquisition is only getting harder and more competitive. To be effective, employers will need to think differently about their definition of talent and further understand their target audience to stand out. As shown in this chapter:

- Talent acquisition needs full C-suite buy-in and support rather than just lip service.

- Existing talent pools are finite and competitive. Employers need to think differently about their definitions of talent to expand them and work strategically to stand out from their competition.

- Employer brand has never been more important. Purpose and story-telling are far more effective than gimmicky benefits, especially post-COVID-19.

- Employers need to build long term relationships with potential hires using data and engagement. They need to demonstrate commitment to and understanding of the communities they are hiring from.

- The future of recruitment marketing is data-driven and personalized.

Endnotes

1 The Conference Board. Press Release: In 2019, CEOs are Most Concerned About Talent and a Recession, www.conference-board.org/pdf_free/press/Press%20Release%20--%20C-Suite%20Challenge%202019.pdf (archived at https://perma.cc/LZZ4-VWTG)

2 Annual Global CEO Survey, 2019, PWC

3 M Alder. Recruiting Future. Ep 190: Building A Disruption Mindset (podcast) 5 June 2019. rfpodcast.com/2019/06/ep-190-building-a-disruption-mindset/ (archived at https://perma.cc/H4T6-W9XB)

4 M Alder. Recruiting Future. Ep 190: Building A Disruption Mindset (podcast) 5 June 2019. rfpodcast.com/2019/06/ep-190-building-a-disruption-mindset/ (archived at https://perma.cc/9KCZ-2EMR)

5 Gartner. Competing for Talent in the Digital Age, www.gartner.com/en/executive-guidance/2017-q3-edition (archived at https://perma.cc/MA2V-CD3C)

6 Gartner. Most Competitive Roles for 2019, www.gartner.com/en/human-resources/research/talentneuron/most-competitive-roles-19?utm_medium=press-release&utm_campaign=RM_GB_2019_CTN_WT_LP1_MOST-COMPETITIVE&utm_term=whitepaper (archived at https://perma.cc/8WAG-7DR4)

7 M Alder. Recruiting Future. Ep 150: Are We Good Enough? (podcast) 6 October 2018. rfpodcast.com/2018/10/ep-150-are-we-good-enough/ (archived at https://perma.cc/H93E-26PS)

8 S Vozza. Why This Tech Company Hires People With No Experience, Fast Company, 28 February 2017. www.fastcompany.com/3068451/why-this-tech-company-hires-people-with-no-experience (archived at https://perma.cc/U2L9-G52F)

9 M Alder. *Recruiting Future*. Ep: 172 Talent for Digital Transformation (podcast) 6 March 2019. rfpodcast.com/2019/03/ep-172-talent-for-digital-transformation/ (archived at https://perma.cc/7SQM-ZNRE)

10 F Gino (2018) *Rebel Talent: Why it pays to break the rules at work and in life*, Dey Street Books, New York, NY

11 M Alder. *Recruiting Future*. Ep: 122: Talent Intelligence (podcast) 28 March 2018. rfpodcast.com/2018/03/ep-122-talent-intelligence/ (archived at https://perma.cc/TDP8-JDHQ)

12 Stack Overflow. 2019 Global Developer Insights Report, www.stackoverflowbusiness.com/uk/talent/resources/global-developer-hiring-landscape-2018 (archived at https://perma.cc/R3FB-2WXV)

13 Wikipedia. The Medium is the Message, en.wikipedia.org/wiki/The_medium_is_the_message (archived at https://perma.cc/4YQ8-ZQ5S)

14 Stack Overflow. www.stackoverflowbusiness.com/uk/talent/resources/global-developer-hiring-landscape-2018 (archived at https://perma.cc/UCM9-GNRD)

15 D McClinton. Global Attention Span is Narrowing and Trends Don't Last As Long Study Reveals, *The Guardian*, 17 April 2019. www.theguardian.com/society/2019/apr/16/got-a-minute-global-attention-span-is-narrowing-study-reveals (archived at https://perma.cc/P2AM-E7HF)

16 R Cialdini. *Pre-Suasion: A revolutionary way to influence and persuade* (2017), Simon & Schuster, New York, NY

17 M Alder. *Recruiting Future*. Ep: 166 The Power of Employee Advocacy (podcast) 6 February 2019. recruitingfuture.com/2019/02/ep-166-the-power-of-employee-advocacy/ (archived at https://perma.cc/Q93X-TAPN)

18 M Alder. *Recruiting Future*. Ep: 141 Business Storytelling With Shane Snow (podcast). recruitingfuture.com/2018/08/ep-141-business-storytelling-with-shane-snow/ (archived at https://perma.cc/J64G-BU3B)

19 M Alder. *Recruiting Future*. Ep: 174 Acquiring Digital Talent (podcast) 14 March 2019. recruitingfuture.com/2019/03/ep-174-acquiring-digital-talent/ (archived at https://perma.cc/8NWB-4X4L)

20 M Alder. *Recruiting Future*. Ep: 131 Inbound Recruiting (podcast) 8 June 2018. recruitingfuture.com/2018/06/ep-131-inbound-recruiting/ (archived at https://perma.cc/33W2-48S4)

21 M Alder. *Recruiting Future*. Ep: 131 Inbound Recruiting (podcast) 8 June 2018. rfpodcast.com/2018/06/ep-131-inbound-recruiting/ (archived at https://perma.cc/D8LR-4ZJL)

22 M Alder. *Recruiting Future*. Ep: 184 Strategic Recruiting (podcast) 11 May 2019. recruitingfuture.com/2019/05/ep-184-strategic-recruiting/ (archived at https://perma.cc/EXS4-B4A5)

23 The Firm. *Insight*, www.thefirm-network.com/insight/ (archived at https://perma.cc/Q3SV-YDQ2)

03

The digital talent experience

Our businesses now survive and grow in what is sometimes referred to as a 'new age of customer capitalism'.[1] The expression, originally from Roger Martin, Dean of Toronto's Rotman School of Management,[2] hinted at a move away from the traditional era of shareholder capitalism into a business climate in which the consumer, customer or client was the top priority. Such an approach maximizes shareholder value by putting customers first, thereby increasing profits and ensuring sustainable business growth and success.

The consumer is now king and queen with their expectations of a flawless experience from every interaction with any company shaped by ever-evolving technology. As Ipsos Mori said 'This means the same kind of immediacy, personalization and convenience that only the elite Customer Experience front-runners such as Google and Amazon have achieved'. This is enhanced through mobile apps for each stage of a process, subscription or transaction, which offer them personalized and intuitive choices and options. The seamless experience they have when shopping, banking, accessing news, checking in for flights, ordering home deliveries and sharing messages and photos with friends, is one they expect in every digital interface. And this includes the workplace, perfectly summed up by Brian Kropp (VP of Gartner) in a quote we have already used earlier in this book – 'Employees want their 9 to 5 to resemble their 5 to 9. And employees' 5 to 9 lives are full of seamless, effortless experiences, largely enabled by digital technologies'. This expectation extends beyond their life at work, and now shapes how they look for new jobs too. In our previous book, *Exceptional Talent,* we looked at the way the employee experience is now playing a key role in the attraction and retention of the talent that businesses need. More information is now freely available to help job seekers better understand what companies are like to work for, primarily through social media channels such as Twitter, Facebook and LinkedIn, all of which are also used by organizations to showcase their working environments. Most job seekers now look beyond the traditional channels and the more corporate style spin and messaging to try and gain more meaningful and personal insights from their broader networks and connections.

While digital technology, the internet and word of mouth all help today's job seekers and workers to find out more about what businesses are really like to work for, the organizations themselves are now also accepting that people have more choices over how and where they work, and who they do that work with. What some may now consider a tired old cliche, the 'war for talent' might have underpinned approaches to hiring for most of the 1990s and early 2000s – primarily by concentrating on how we went about the process of acquisition rather than identifying the profile of the person who would fit best – but the focus is now on being a place where people want to work. If there is a 'battle' for talent, it is now over being the place where people can achieve whatever they want.

As discussed, whether you are going to a restaurant, shopping online, enjoying a holiday or choosing a new car, the customer experience is paramount, and most business planning around new products, services and journeys is done accordingly. What we offer our customers, we now need to offer our employees. Digital talent expects nothing less! An important reason for this is that all our employees, job candidates, contingent labour and freelancers are customers too. Businesses worked out some time ago that their customers are not just end-users, but people with needs, emotions and a desire for connection, so it is time to adopt and apply the same thinking to the employee lifecycle. The link between how someone is treated by an organization during the hiring process – from application to offer – and whether they continue to buy from them as customers, has been recognized as one of the driving factors behind the shaping of the candidate experience. A frequently quoted case study involving Virgin Media from 2015 found that rejected candidates, who went on to cancel their subscriptions after being rejected, cost the business in excess of £4 million a year. Reputation was also damaged, as 18% of rejected candidates were identified as 'detractors' on the Net Promoter Score (NPS) scale, meaning they were unlikely to recommend the brand to others.

Digital talent is now much more in control of the job search, with expectations of a seamless, intuitive, informed, consumer-style experience. It's what we refer to as the digital talent experience and, in this chapter, we will explore many of the expectations, preferences and concerns that drive this. The first thing we need to stress about this experience is that it is not concerned with any one specific part of the talent journey. We may talk about different stages of this journey, about application experience, candidate experience, hiring experience, employee experience and learning experience, but when we talk about talent experience, we mean the whole journey – from awareness of the organization to maintaining alumni relations: the experience that employees get will define their relationship with you.

Digital talent challenges

Before we delve into the talent experience itself, we need to consider the recruitment marketplace today. Businesses looking to hire and retain digital talent have a number of challenges to overcome. First, they need to look carefully at their pipelines of future skills and future leadership. Do they have people already in the business who can grow, develop and move into new roles? Or are they going to try to hire people externally who can join and have the potential to grow and develop within the business? This is key, as there is a shortage of digital skills globally, made worse by the exponential pace of change and digital transformation.

Second, the concept of talent itself needs to be redefined. Historically, we have looked at the career histories of job candidates and usually hire someone who has already performed a similar role elsewhere. Now we need to hire not for the job as it is today, but for the job that it will become, and find ways to attract and assess for development potential. As well as skills and achievements already attained, we need to hire for business capabilities, which are often not apparent from CVs or standard interview questioning.

Third, retention of talent itself has become a key consideration. As we will see later, retention need not only mean that an employee stays with you in the long term, but that you retain a relationship with them. They may wish to work with you again in a different capacity, possibly in a freelance arrangement, and they may also be able to recommend future candidates for your vacancies. The increase in using external hiring, as opposed to internal promotion, to fill roles that we have seen in recent decades has created a situation where companies expect employee turnover, yet still need to invest in training and development that they may not see direct long-term benefits from.

As hiring becomes more competitive, we have seen greater expectations for new hires to perform quickly. This has put the spotlight firmly on onboarding, which, as we will explore later, has now become much more digital, beginning before an offer has even been made, and continuing well past the first three months of employment.

The fourth major challenge is that job seekers themselves are now much better informed, checking companies before they apply, forming a view on the type of organization they are to work for, the opportunities for development, and trying to get a feel for the culture. They don't only look at the information that an organization puts out about itself but will read reviews and search online, using search engines to find stories from people who are working there or have previously worked there. For example, 'I used to work at ...' or 'When I worked at ...' are popular Google searches when job-hunting. As only around one in five employees see a strong alignment between what the employer says about itself and the actual experience of working there,[3] and it has become so simple and important for employees to understand as much as possible about a company, organizations should be paying close attention to every aspect of the experience for current and former employees as well.

And finally, career expectations have also changed. Purpose and meaning are important when choosing where to work, as is finding a culture that encourages connection and collaboration, innovation and experimentation. People want to work somewhere that supports and enables them to learn, grow, develop and achieve, while recognizing and rewarding their work. And, as we have just outlined in the opening of the chapter, organizations must factor in the consumer-led expectations of the talent experience, ensuring they have a seamless hiring and onboarding process.

Understanding the talent experience

It's unlikely that any job candidate ever says to themselves, 'I really enjoyed the interviewing, can't wait to see what the onboarding will be like' or once hired 'that performance management review was really good, wonder how effective my digital learning will be', but every interaction with, and within, the organization consistently creates expectations for future ones. From the company's viewpoint, there are a number of separate interactions and interventions along the employment journey, each with different stakeholders, but from the employee's view, there is just one journey within one organization. As Laura Stevens, predictive people analytics expert at Deloitte, said in Autumn 2020 'Employees look at everything that happens at work as an integrated experience, and expect businesses to operate as one seamless organization'. With most of their personal lives operating seamlessly, our employees expect their working lives to be the same.

Research in 2019 from Bersin by Deloitte also described talent management as a 'networked, customizable system with individuals – and their relationship with the organization-at the centre' and found that employers who see it as a collection of individual transactions and events tend to lose competitive advantage. This means that the overall talent experience we are writing about is the result of how all the overlapping recruiting and HR processes are able to manifest as a single ongoing journey. Seamless and consistent experiences take time to create. For the overall talent experience the internal employee touchpoints we need to consider include recruitment/talent acquisition, hiring managers, senior management and leadership, HR and learning and analytics. Unsurprisingly, one of the stumbling blocks to creating a seamless work experience we regularly find from our research is that each stage of the talent cycle has different stakeholders who are rarely able to offer a consistent approach. For example, the hiring phase may be primarily under the remit of the recruitment or talent acquisition team, while onboarding is usually overseen by a combination of HR, learning and development and line managers. If the talent lifecycle were viewed as a relay race, then this first changeover usually sees the baton dropped more often than not. Any inconsistency in the quality of experience and interactions between different stakeholders during onboarding will immediately frustrate a new hire. They have navigated hiring and have a good feeling about the organization they have just joined, yet if the key phase that starts their employment delivers a poor experience, and most importantly, doesn't set them up for a successful start, they begin with a negative experience.

In late 2019 we partnered with recruitment tech business Saba (now part of CornerstoneInc) to survey recruitment and HR professionals and get more insight into how they saw the talent experience. Starting with the recruitment experience, we found over 90% of respondents were aware of how important the quality of this experience was, with over half admitting they were working hard to improve it. One key issue identified was to ensure that HR and the hiring managers had a good experience themselves to be able to offer the same to candidates. Processes, teams and systems need to work effectively and in alignment or else building a good experience for candidates and employees is unlikely to happen.

From our interviews, it became apparent that most businesses were aware of the importance of creating a process that enabled candidates to progress smoothly through the hiring process, thereby ensuring consistency of experience at each stage, and they also knew that a positive recruitment experience will create the expectation of a positive employee experience once hired. This was supported by the project's quantitative survey, in which we found 87% agreeing that the recruitment experience must reflect the employee experience. However, the reality is that firms struggle in this area with only one in six believing they were actually able to achieve this consistency of experience, while almost a third admitted that there were significant differences. Maintaining consistency between the recruitment experience and employee experience is critical. Without it, there is a danger of candidates being mis-sold roles, or not understanding what life will be like inside a new organization, both of which are key reasons behind the early attrition of new hires, something we will be exploring in a later section.

The importance of speed and information when hiring

First impressions count when hiring, so it is important to remember that the candidate experience phase of the talent experience begins long before a first interview. Potential candidates hear of roles through advertising, word of mouth and searching online. The employer brand touchpoints range from social media to recommendations from ex-employees, and all need to be consistent and positive. Potential applicants will use these to try and determine if they think both the role and the organization are right for them. Almost 40% of businesses we surveyed with Saba admitted that job seekers get a poor experience of trying to research their business, brand and offering.

Looking at the transition from candidate to a new hire, our research found around 80% of companies believe they give a high-quality experience at the offer stage, but once they get an acceptance, the quality drops, as we have already mentioned earlier in the previous section. Just under 60% rated their onboarding experience as being of high quality and less than half (47%) felt their overall pre-joining experience was good enough. Let that sink in for a moment. We've ensured that our candidates have a good experience when being hired, yet once they've accepted, the quality of their experience drops. I think most readers will agree that this is unacceptable, yet it happens on a regular basis.

The way we help people settle into our businesses will determine how well they perform, develop and contribute. Back in 2018, I watched a conference presentation from a consulting business that worked with smaller organizations to help them improve their candidate and hiring experiences. They ran a project with a small number of SME businesses in which they had tracked candidates who had applied for roles right through to them either being rejected or being hired and found out how they felt at each stage of the candidate experience journey. This was tracked from the first awareness of a vacancy, through application and screening, interviews, offer or rejection, notice period, and their first three months after joining. At each stage they asked candidates how they felt about the organization that they were trying to join, using the net promoter score. At each stage, candidates rated four specific areas – how engaged they felt, the speed with which things were happening, how respected they felt and the level of information that they were getting from the company. Incredibly, what this research showed was that the two points on the entire journey at which candidates felt least engaged with the business were in-between their first and second interview, and while they were working their notice period having accepted an offer, surely the two stages when the hiring company needs them to feel most engaged. Further analysis showed that these were the two points of the journey at which candidates also felt that the information they were receiving was not enough for what they wanted, being either non-existent or insufficient. That point is worth repeating; while they are preparing for their second interview, and while they are waiting to join the company, candidates and new hires are not getting the information they need. Additionally, these two stages of the journey were also the ones at which they felt that the process was moving too slowly. There are important lessons to be learned for all organizations from this small research project, namely that the information candidates receive, and the speed with which things happen during the early part of the talent experience lifecycle, are both hugely important. If things don't happen smoothly, we clearly risk alienating new hires before they've even joined us. The best way to ensure a talent experience that is both consistent and of high quality is to personalize it, and research shows that it is this personalization that really creates a winning experience. It is vitally important that businesses work with their employees, and their prospective employees, to understand the moments that really matter to them most. Getting this feedback is crucial to understanding what the different segments of the talent marketplace want in order to build memorable moments of experience, which will ultimately help create personalized user journeys for them, where they can feel more in control.

The real employee experience

When we talk about the employee experience it is usually framed from the company's viewpoint. Hence for many leaders, it might be a great reward and benefits scheme, or system of recognition. It might even encompass the latest technology, open approaches to flexible and hybrid working, and any number of HR initiatives to improve employees' lives at work. For example, on the latter point, research shows that one in three[4] would quit their job if they felt the technology they are using is outdated, and three-quarters need to have an opportunity for professional development to feel satisfied in their job, so any HR intervention aimed at addressing those might be seen as improving the engagement and retention.

Glossy employer branding videos that show a diverse range of happy employees gathered around the latest office coffee machine or brainstorming while sitting on bean bags may have been popular a few years ago but things seem to have changed. The expectations many jobseekers have from new employers are around growth, development, opportunity and meaning, not creature comforts. The working environment is important but is driven by connection and collaboration with colleagues rather than relaxation zones. When we shape employee experience from the organizational perspective, we miss out on what is most important to employees, namely the myriad of everyday experiences and interactions that shape their life at work and combine to create the lived employee experience. These were recognized in OC Tanner's 2020 *Global Culture Report*[5] as 'the personal, every day, career-defining, micro-experiences that shape life at work'. These experiences can comprise hundreds of daily interactions employees have with colleagues, management, technology, clients… and yes, the office coffee machine! They are all integral to creating an engaging employee experience. In fact, 92% of employees surveyed told OC Tanner that they see the employee experience as their everyday experience. For them, the employee experience is a human experience and only 42% rated it as positive. As Laura Stevens from Deloitte said in 2020:[6] 'Employee experience is not about what actually happened; rather, it's about what is perceived, understood and remembered by the employee'. In recent years much has been written about the evolution of the employee experience, not least by the author and futurist Jacob Morgan, whose research has charted three phases in the evolution of employee experience. The first can be called the 'utility' phase in which the focus is on providing employees with the basic essential tools they need to work effectively, such as a desk, chair, phone and computer. The next evolution addressed what was needed to help employees work harder and faster and to become more productive. This involved improved approaches from leaders, support and development, and the operational processes and technology that helps support them. The final evolution brings us to employee engagement as we understand it today, which is more concerned with culture and making employees happy and connected with their work, engaged with the organization, and inspired to achieve results. Initially achieved by using tools such as annual surveys and mission statements, this has now developed into a number of initiatives such as reward and recognition programmes that bring a human and personal element to the workplace.

Despite companies striving to improve these experiences, OC Tanner's 2020 *Global Culture Report* found only 66% of all employees believing that their employee experience mattered to their organizations,[7] while Deloitte's reported 84% of employees saying that employee experience was an important issue for their companies to improve,[8] with a third rating it one of their organization's top three urgent issues to address. This is important because research shows that almost 20% of employees – primarily younger employees – quit jobs in 2017 due to a poor employee experience,[9] and there is little doubt that this figure has been increasing. One important reason why the employee experience often fails to deliver is that while many organizations listen to their workers – either through formal and informal conversations or digital listening tools that read the sentiment of internal employee interactions – they do not always take action. Research in 2020 from people success platform Glint found that employees who do not believe their company will act on their feedback are seven times more likely to be disengaged than those who do.[10] When it comes to employee experience, actions speak louder than intentions.

The importance of micro-experiences

When we talk about the talent experience being a number of interlocking processes and events, it should be considered that, from the employee perspective, this doesn't simply cover the initiatives established by HR, talent acquisition or business leaders, but smaller interlocking events within those, and each one has a series of micro experiences. For example, let's look at onboarding. For your new hire, this may be their first experience of how the organization really operates on a day-to-day basis, and hence a very early part of the talent lifecycle. As a standard process, onboarding will include offer management – primarily how the offer is structured and communicated – the information given, acceptance (either in-person or virtually) and how that acceptance was received. It will also be about the welcome – is it by email or letter – and are they being given access to technology that tells them what they need to know about the organization before they start. Can they meet the team virtually, are there culture interviews to watch, and a virtual tour of any office or workspace? The first day at work itself contains many more experiences from an orientation of the workspace, physically meeting the team and everyone else who will be part of their day-to-day life at work, learning more about organizational purpose, finding out about the technology they'll be using plus the initial experiences of actually using it. Understanding policies, procedures and finding out where the coffee machine is, and so on. And then there is the possibility of getting a first assignment or project to work on. All of these micro-experiences, some lasting only seconds, will determine whether you get off to a good or bad start, and will also shape the first impressions of a new employer. The importance of the impact of these experiences cannot be underestimated.

In their best-selling book, *The Power of Moments*,[11] Doctors Chip and Dan Heath write about the impact of positive or 'peak' experiences and negative or 'valley' experiences, showing that the positive benefits of a 'peak' experience can last up to four weeks, while the negative impact of a 'valley' experience lasts two weeks. Although it is shorter, the negative experience might initially seem to have a deeper and more immediate impact. However, peak experiences tend to be accompanied by stronger and more positive emotions, meaning they are more memorable in the longer term. Relating these findings to the employee journey, peak experiences can serve as signposts along the way and are the kind of experiences we will share with colleagues, friends, family and people within our personal networks. Yet most of the time HR, line managers and business leaders try to deal with minimizing the negative experiences, attempting to smooth them out and make sure they don't happen. As the impact of a positive experience lasts much longer than the negative impact of a poor experience does, instead of focusing too hard on ironing out the negative moments, our teams need to focus on how to create an increasing number of positive moments. Of course, the key to great experiences is usually found in workplace culture. If the culture is one that supports, enables and engages then this impacts how employees think, act and interact, creating more peak micro experiences, which then reinforce a positive workplace culture. Organizations need to work closely with their employees to ascertain the moments that really matter the most and ensure that they can amplify and maximize the experience.

From a job for life to external hiring

So far, we have been talking about the experiences new employees get during the hiring and induction phases, but we also need to pause and consider why the roles we are filling need to be hired externally. After all, being a great place to work also implies you offer chances for progression and development. As Peter Cappelli, Wharton School of Management concluded in his research paper from 2019[12] 'Businesses have never done as much hiring as they do today. They've never spent as much money doing it. And they've never done a worse job of it.'

Countless surveys of HR and business leaders consistently find their top concerns to be the quality of their future talent pipeline, having access to the skills they need to be competitive, and the calibre of their future management pool. The vast majority also complain that it is difficult to hire the people they need. Clearly, there are reasons for this, not least that hiring managers have become very specific about the skills, experience and potential that they want to hire, even if they don't always have the assessment and screening processes in place to deliver them. Companies are hiring external candidates more than at any time in the past, in fact, less than 30% of recruitment leaders say that internal candidates are an important source when filling new positions. Perhaps the most damning statistic in recent years came from the Deloitte Global Human Capital Trends survey of 2019 where almost 60% of employees said that it is easier to find a new role in another business than to move within their existing business.[13] It wasn't always this way so how has it come to this? Looking back from the end of World War Two, through to the 1980s – what we think of as the 'job for life' era – the majority of organizations filled new positions from within. Research indicates that roughly 90% of vacancies were filled through promotions and lateral assignments within the organization. Today, less than a third of positions are filled in this way, which aligns with the perception of employees cited in the previous paragraph.

Anybody starting work in the 1970s or 1980s would no doubt have worked with, and reported to, people who had been with their organizations for a long time and had 'worked their way up'. Certainly, when Mervyn was working for an accountancy firm in the early 1980s, he found that most of the firm's managers were people who had started as trainees and worked their way through the different levels of audit senior, supervisor and manager. The lucky few would eventually be made partners. Almost all the partners' secretaries had started as either filing clerks or in the typing pool, and the firm invested in their development, usually paying for external courses to enable them to improve their skills and better themselves. Even though current research shows that the primary reason somebody will join and stay, with an organization is if they have the chance to grow, develop and learn new skills, something has changed to result in the increase in external hiring. Perhaps organizations do not fully invest in this, despite what they might describe and offer during the hiring process.

This also creates increased competition in the recruitment market. Effectively companies are hiring from competitors, who themselves then hire from competitors, and so on, creating a revolving cycle of people moving on. Our own 2020 research with Actus Software[14] backs this up, as we found 62% of HR managers saying that people leave their organizations to take up jobs that could have been offered to them internally, with only 6% looking to fill new vacancies internally in the first instance.

The research focused on companies in the USA showing that 95% of hiring is done to fill existing positions, most being created by the voluntary turnover of people leaving to take jobs elsewhere. One of the most puzzling aspects of this study[15] by Matthew Bidwell and Peter Cappelli of Wharton School of Management was that it found external hires taking up to three years to perform as well in a role as an internal hire moving through an internal transfer, while the internal hire takes up to seven years to earn as much as an external hire earns for doing the same job. High levels of external hiring disrupt culture and lower engagement as existing employees see their career paths blocked so they will devote time and energy to looking elsewhere. Gradually the spotlight is turning towards internal mobility, in other words filling new roles with the people you already have. This has gradually been moving towards the top of the HR agenda for the last few years, and certainly, the hiring freezes that arose from the COVID-19 pandemic helped to accelerate this. We will be looking at internal mobility in greater detail later, in Chapter 4, but suffice to say that when new vacancies arise, all businesses need to start looking internally.

The cost of employee attrition

It is easy to see why some managers look to hire externally. New people can bring fresh ideas and experiences, might look at problems and planning from a different angle, and will probably bring energy and enthusiasm as they try to prove themselves to new employers. On the downside, they may take time to get up to speed or properly understand the culture and working environment of their new role or could need more training than expected. And, as we have just mentioned, a new arrival may lead to established employees losing enthusiasm for their business and becoming less productive, particularly if they feel that their options for progression have become limited. A further downside to external hiring is that at least 25% of new hires leave within the first six months,[16] further impacting morale and productivity. Up to 90% of external hires admit to using their experience of the first six months to decide on whether to commit themselves to the business long term. The early days of employment are a much-researched period. As far back as 2013, research from Corporate Executive Board (now a division of Gartner) concluded that around one in five hires turn out to be bad, or regretted decisions, while training business Leadership IQ concluded that two out of every five external appointments turn out to be bad hires within the first 18 months.[17] There are several potential costs associated with hires who leave within the first few months. Firstly, there is the salary paid to that employee for the time they were with the business during which they had quite possibly been underperforming. There might also be some contractual payments around bonuses or team performance. Any investment in training may well have not been recouped by performance, and crucially there is a negative impact on team morale and external reputation if new employees join and leave within a short space of time. To this, you may need to add an increase in sickness or absence, both of which are fairly common among employees who find that they've made a poor decision when joining a company. While some of these may be difficult to quantify, Gallup estimates that actively disengaged employees in the US cost businesses between $450 billion and $550 billion annually in lost productivity.[18]

Summarizing a number of research studies over the years, the main reasons that new hires don't settle include:

1 The job wasn't what they expected from the hiring process.
2 They don't get on with their manager or team.
3 Company culture isn't one they feel comfortable with.
4 They see no scope for development or progression.
5 Their skills and knowledge are being under-utilized.

These factors often arise from a combination of circumstances. These may include over-enthusiastic hiring managers who will often try to fill a role quickly once they see a suitable candidate, rushed and muddled interview processes that don't let the candidate see as much of the culture and organization as they would like, and poor onboarding.

Organizations looking to hire and engage digital talent need to adopt an approach to attraction, interviewing, onboarding and talent management that lets prospective candidates know exactly what to expect when they join and that supports them in becoming successful and productive employees. We will now start exploring ways (in the rest of this chapter and the next) in which this can happen, particularly in light of the events of 2020 when new hires were not having physical interviews, nor visiting the places where they would be working nor meeting their new colleagues and managers. Yet over three-quarters were happy to accept a role without that, as long as they had all the insights needed to make a decision, including videos, photos and culture interviews. The talent experience can be and should be designed in such a way that it can give them all the information and insights needed to make those decisions without seeing people and places 'in person'.

The role of hiring managers

One of the key stakeholders right through the recruitment phase of the talent experience is the hiring manager. We have seen in the last two sections that their desire to fill gaps in their teams with fully rounded, experienced employees often leads to either a hiring mistake or to someone leaving because they see a lack of opportunity. With digital talent looking for companies that can support their growth and development, we need hiring managers who can embody the talent experience and inspire their new hires. To put it bluntly, having effective hiring managers is crucial for businesses looking to hire and develop the talent they need. It is crucial for job candidates too. Over 90% say that the impression they get of the person they will be working for will most influence their decision on whether to join and, as we have just seen, one of the key factors causing early employee attrition is an inability to get on with their line manager. We have previously mentioned that hiring managers have become very specific about the skills, experience and potential that they want to hire. In the first half of 2020, we undertook a large research project on hiring manager effectiveness, across all sectors, to try and understand the reality of the experience candidates get when meeting them and looking at ways in which companies could try and improve it. There clearly is an issue as 49% of the talent acquisition and HR professionals we surveyed said that their hiring managers were not effective at offering a good candidate experience, with around 40% also saying that they weren't able to accurately represent the employer brand or employer value proposition (EVP) either. This could be down to organizational culture issues as only a third said that the quality of experience that candidates get throughout the hiring phase is important to their senior business leadership. Overall, we found an almost 'us versus them' mentality between the recruitment and HR teams, and hiring managers, which results in a muddled candidate experience. Hiring managers appear to have little input into the recruitment process design, and there are times during the interviewing and assessment process when different stakeholders get involved. For example, when looking at who takes responsibility for outlining to candidates the potential for career growth and skill development, which is one of the key reasons why they would join the organization, we found that while hiring managers discuss this most often, this only happens within just over a third of the companies we spoke to. At different times the talent acquisition team, HR, learning and development and even senior leaders all get involved in this conversation. To have this multitude of stakeholders combining over a key, and very personal, part of the employment offering can only risk confusing candidates and weaken the message.

There is also a split between the hiring manager, the talent acquisition team and HR when it comes to making the offer to a successful candidate. Given some of the points we've already raised about the early stages of the talent experience, it's crucial that there is consistency in how potential hires receive their offers. If they have built up a good rapport with the hiring manager who has interviewed them, then it should be that person who makes the offer. In reality, hiring is not a constant behaviour for hiring managers. Unlike the talent acquisition and HR teams, a hiring manager doesn't have an ongoing overview of the recruitment marketplace, which includes understanding which skills are in demand and which candidates might be available. This leads to them thinking that a vacancy can be filled relatively simply by interviewing a shortlist of candidates eager to join. Clearly, this isn't the way modern recruiting works, so hiring managers need to be brought into the process design a lot more. Recruitment and HR leaders must work closely with all their hiring managers to both educate them on the changing trends in the talent marketplace and also involve them in designing both the candidate experience and EVP, making sure that they are able to give these values to the candidates who will work for them.

What do candidates really think about the candidate experience?

In our 2018 research project conducted among 14,000 European jobseekers, we found that for over half of them the top factor influencing their decision to apply for a role was how a company treats its staff. For the UK this figure was almost two-thirds. This reason was some way ahead of the second most popular reason, which was the company's ambition and growth plans. Some of the factors that are traditionally thought to be influential – such as financial benefits, culture and approaches to diversity – were ranked much lower. This isn't to say that these factors don't have influence, but it's more likely to be on the decision to accept an offer rather than to apply in the first place. There were two other factors prompting an application if there was a vacancy of interest that are worth a mention. The work the company does, and the opportunity to make a contribution, was important to almost 40%. As well as being a great place to work, you also need to be able to offer the purpose and meaning we referenced earlier. One of the lower-ranking factors was having the opportunity to work flexibly, however, we think it's fairly safe to assume that for 2020 and beyond this will increase in significance.

We can't stress enough the importance of how you treat candidates during the application and hiring process to whether or not your vacancies are filled. In the opening to this chapter, we referenced a study that involved Virgin Media to evidence why the candidate experience is so important in the longer term, but for filling immediate hiring needs it is also crucial as, without a good experience, candidates are much less likely to join you. In fact, our research study found 87% of job seekers saying that the way they are treated during the application and interview stages will impact their decision on whether to join. Almost a third will drop out at the interview stage if they don't like the way they are being treated, are unimpressed by their interviewers or think the process is taking too long. Throughout the process, they will consistently check online reviews and do their own further research on the role. Additionally, anecdotes around poor recruitment experiences are shared widely by candidates on social media, particularly on platforms such as LinkedIn. A negative experience shared is most likely to deter future candidates from applying. How do job applicants find out what you are like to work for? Well, for around two-thirds it is online reviews and other people's opinions that are most influential. In fact, only 6% of the 14,000 candidates we surveyed said that these had no influence whatsoever.

Digital businesses need to be consistently monitoring social media platforms to see what is being said about them, and about their hiring processes.

The online application itself should take around five to ten minutes. If it's shorter, then candidates are concerned that they may not have given enough information and if it takes longer, then over half of them will drop out. Over a third find some of the questions during an application process confusing or irrelevant, and a similar proportion will drop out if your recruitment technology is too slow or unresponsive. To protect your organization's reputation, and keep a good applicant flow, members of the talent acquisition and HR teams should regularly apply for their own jobs to check the experience for themselves. Candidates get frustrated with the length of the process and how many steps and interview stages there are, while one in five complained that often the person interviewing them isn't prepared and hasn't read the information that has already been submitted. For the UK, around 35% withdraw from the process because they are not impressed by the attitude or manner of either their interviewer or the recruiter who screened them. Over 80% expect just a two or three-stage recruiting process. The application is seen as the first stage followed by just one or two interviews. The third stage would be some form of skills assessment. The biggest frustration of all though is around feedback. Over half complained about a lack of feedback on application outcomes. This is not post-interview. This is on the outcome of an application that has effectively disappeared into the ether and about which they hear nothing more, leaving them unsure of whether they have been rejected or not even considered. It leaves them unsure on whether or not to accept another offer (in case they hear back) and results in them feeling undervalued and not having their experience properly recognized. Why is this important? It's because, as we have already said, for almost 90% of job seekers it's the way they are treated during the application and interview process that will determine whether they accept an offer. The only other factors of similar importance are their impressions of the manager they will be working for, and the opportunities they see for growth and development, which is also their number one expectation from a new employer over the first two years of employment (we will discuss this latter point further in Chapter 4 when we look at talent management).

How your talent experience helps you to attract and hire the talent you need

The expected seamless and integrated nature of the talent experience means that the talent acquisition team cannot operate in isolation but needs to adapt their role and focus on the whole employee lifecycle, partnering with HR to create the journey digital talent expects. Most advice aimed at helping recruiters to better achieve their goals tends to look at what the recruitment team can do for itself. However, as we have seen, digital talent needs to know more, so the talent acquisition team cannot just focus on their application and interviewing processes but, with the help of HR, they have to look at their role in delivering the overall talent experience cycle.

This means a number of things. First, that talent acquisition teams need to be much more open about future development paths. Rather than trying to fill specific roles against tight deadlines, they need to be able to talk to candidates about their longer-term opportunities if they join the business, sharing the overall business vision. Second, they also need to promote creative flexible working solutions; 2020 saw a huge shift in how and where people work, but this is a trend that had already begun. Certainly, a significant number of the job seekers that we surveyed in 2018 were looking to join companies that could support and enable them to work more flexibly, and this opportunity now needs to be part of the overall hiring offering. The talent acquisition team needs to be much more forward-facing and when they are looking to fill a role, they should hire for the role that it will become and not the one it has been and is today. This means looking ahead and working with hiring managers to forecast the kind of skills and capabilities that might be either necessary or desirable as the role develops and mapping out how these can be either found or developed.

It isn't necessary to recruit people who fit a tight job specification now but to find people who have the ability to grow as the role develops. The talent acquisition team also have to see themselves as part of the onboarding process, and not a stakeholder who can pass the baton to HR or learning and development once an offer has been accepted. Onboarding starts as early as the first or second interview as new hires see their process of joining a business beginning much earlier than the day they physically start. We saw in an earlier section that the quality and speed of the information flow during the recruitment process has a hugely significant impact on how someone settles in once they start.

We've also talked earlier in this section about hiring manager effectiveness. The talent acquisition team needs to look at how they partner with hiring managers and help them to fully understand the talent marketplace and the desires and expectations of candidates they interview. This also includes involving them in the recruitment process design (possibly co-creating it with them) and also in making sure that hiring managers have input to the development of EVP and employer brand.

Should candidates be rejected, then the way this is done will have a great impact on future hiring. Stories of a poor candidate experience spread quickly through digital channels, not least when feedback is weak or non-existent. Teams now pay attention to what is known as the 'journey of regret', which is the overall experience of letting candidates know they haven't been selected and looking at ways to add value to create a positive candidate experience. This involves looking at ways in which feedback can be provided, and perhaps pointing unsuccessful candidates in the direction of different opportunities or helping them understand how they can acquire and develop the skills and capabilities to be considered again in future.

Overall, the whole recruitment function needs to move on from seeing themselves as filling vacancies to becoming part of an overall business talent strategy, not just recruiting future skill requirements but understanding them and planning for them. This also means knowing how to properly assess candidate strengths and capabilities.

There are a number of innovative assessment approaches such as soft skill assessments, job auditions, virtual reality assessments and video interviews to name but a few that research finds can give a much more realistic and insightful snapshot of a candidate's core capabilities, plus improve predictions of strong post-hire performance. Ultimately, every business needs to be a business where talent can thrive and where people want to work, and everyone involved in the attraction and hiring of future talent has to play their part in being that business.

Chapter summary

Our future employees expect the hiring and onboarding processes to be a series of seamless experiences, much like those they have as consumers. In reality, there are many different stakeholders within these processes, but all must realize the importance of consistency, and much like a relay team, no one can afford to drop the baton by giving a poor or disjointed experience. As we have discussed in this chapter:

- Jobseekers want regular information and feedback during the application, interview and hiring phases. Periods of silence, or rejection without rationale, will create a poor experience and can lead to negative reviews on recruitment sites.

- Understand the micro-experiences and the value of giving as many positive, or peak, experiences as possible during the hiring process. Try to regularly apply for your own jobs and experience all the pre-application and application touchpoints that jobseekers do. Is it good enough?

- Do we really know all the 'moments that matter' to our employees, the ones that shape their employee experience? Find out what they are, listen to what they say, and always look for ways to improve them.

- Be open about future development paths when hiring.

- The talent acquisition team needs to see themselves as part of the overall business talent planning strategy, and not merely vacancy fillers.

Endnotes

1 R L Martin. The Age of Customer Capitalism, *Harvard Business Review*, January–February 2010. hbr.org/2010/01/the-age-of-customer-capitalism, (archived at https://perma.cc/DT9M-CCPK)

2 Cision PRNewswire. Article Calls for the 'Age of Customer Capitalism', 18 January 2010. www.prnewswire.com/news-releases/article-calls-for-the-age-of-customer-capitalism-81984427.html (archived at https://perma.cc/THQ8-8Q4Q)

3 Webershandwick. Only 19 Percent of Employees Globally Report Their Experience At Work Matches Their Organization's Employer Brand, 14 November 2017. www.webershandwick.com/news/only-19-percent-of-employees-globally-report-their-experience-at-work-matches-their-organizations-employer-brand/ (archived at https://perma.cc/VAZ8-J8LB)

4 Ultimate Software. New National Study Uncovers Notable Shift in Factors Influencing Employee Job Satisfaction, Engagement, 4 October 2016. www.ultimatesoftware.com/PR/Press-Release/New-National-Study-Uncovers-Notable-Shift-in-Factors-Influencing-Employee-Job-Satisfaction-Engagement (archived at https://perma.cc/FT89-BXKR)

5 O.C.Tanner. Global Culture 2020 Report, www.octanner.com/au/global-culture-report/2020/experiences.html (archived at https://perma.cc/HVE2-ZUCR)

6 L Nicholas. Unleash Employee Experience: Getting HR Beyond the Buzz Word, 2 October 2020. www.unleashgroup.io/2020/10/02/employee-experience-beyond-the-buzz-towards-business-intelligence/ (archived at https://perma.cc/HQ5M-CU9V)

7 O.C.Tanner. Global Culture 2020 Report, www.octanner.com/au/global-culture-report/2020/experiences.html (archived at https://perma.cc/Z4HZ-GF6Q)

8 E Volini, I Roy, J Schwartz, M Hauptmann, Y Van Durme. Global Human Capital Trends, Deloitte, 11 April 2019. www2.deloitte.com/us/en/insights/focus/human-capital-trends/2019/workforce-engagement-employee-experience.html (archived at https://perma.cc/P2PY-TP9V)

9   O.C. Tanner. Global Culture 2020 Report, www.octanner.com/au/global-culture-report/2020/experiences.html (archived at https://perma.cc/L7QW-CBE6)

10   J Gonzales. When Should Managers Get Access to Survey Results? Sooner Than you Think, *Glint*, 12 November 2019. www.glintinc.com/blog/when-should-managers-get-access-to-employee-engagement-survey-results-sooner-than-you-think/#:~:text=According%20to%20Glint's%20research%2C%20employees,believe%20action%20will%20be%20taken (archived at https://perma.cc/E29L-RQFR).

11   C Heath and D Heath. 2017, *The Power of Moments: Why certain experiences have extraordinary impact*, Simon & Schuster, New York, NY.

12   P Cappelli. Your Approach to Hiring Is All Wrong, *Harvard Business Review* (May–June 2019). hbr.org/2019/05/your-approach-to-hiring-is-all-wrong (archived at https://perma.cc/3UMB-GJEW)

13   Deloitte. Insights Leading the Social Enterprise: Reinvent with Human Focus, 2019 Deloitte Global Human Capital Trends. www2.deloitte.com/content/dam/insights/us/collections/HC-Trends2019/DI_HC-Trends-2019.pdf (archived at https://perma.cc/VJZ4-PK5S)

14   Actus. The Internal Mobility Report: Drive Employee Engagement in 2021, actus.co.uk/free-performance-management-resources/whitepapers/the-internal-mobility-report-drive-employee-engagement-in-2021/ (archived at https://perma.cc/E4ZQ-BHG9)

15   P Cappelli. Your Approach to Hiring Is All Wrong, *Harvard Business Review* (May–June 2019). hbr.org/2019/05/your-approach-to-hiring-is-all-wrong (archived at https://perma.cc/64HV-X8NJ)

16   Recruiting.com. Are Your New Hires Quitting? www.recruiting.com/blog/are-your-new-hires-quitting/ (archived at https://perma.cc/8H6H-HVYL)

17   REC. Perfect match Making the right hire and the cost of getting it wrong, 2017. www.rec.uk.com/our-view/research/recruitment-insights/perfect-match-making-right-hire-and-cost-getting-it-wrong (archived at https://perma.cc/4G6A-G2TU)

18   S Sorenson and K Garman. How to Tackle US Employees' Stagnating Engagement, Gallup, 11 June 2013. news.gallup.com/businessjournal/162953/tackle-employees-stagnating-engagement.aspx (archived at https://perma.cc/AYQ9-A8BP)

04

New thinking around talent management

There is a growing realization that for the modern HR professional one of the key areas in which they can add most commercial value to the business, supporting it in the achievement of commercial goals, is in talent management. The very nature of digital transformation requires all organizations to have a workforce that is constantly up-skilling and learning, supported in their development, that feels free to experiment and innovate and feels happy, engaged recognized and rewarded.

In their 2020 Report on Jobs[1], the World Economic Forum said, 'for those workers set to remain in their roles, the share of core skills that will change in the next 5 years is 40%, and 50% of all employees will need reskilling'. Meanwhile, LinkedIn's 2018 talent research[2] showed that half of the most in-demand skills were not even on the list three years earlier.

We have seen in the previous chapter how a business's ability to show that they can offer opportunities for upskilling and reskilling is key to hiring the talent they need, so it falls on the HR team to ensure that there is a culture and environment for this to happen.

Historical approaches to talent management have centred on the hierarchical organizational structure, with rigid promotion lines, training delivered by the business at times they set, and annual performance reviews with direct (and usually one-way) feedback which in turn are linked to salary and bonus reviews. When new skills, a touch more dynamism or a different perspective were needed, they tended to be hired in from outside. From trainee positions onwards there were stages of development that had to be achieved to move on to the next level. Employees were developed by gradually giving them more complex work projects or additional responsibilities. With correct supervision, they began to learn the skills and capabilities they needed to move on to the next level of the organizational structure. The roles they were aspiring to move on to usually were those being performed by the people managing them.

The digital workplace is different. Previously we were thinking in terms of jobs and our people were looking to move to the next level of their job, but now it isn't about the job or the role – it's about skills. The business of tomorrow will not be based on creating jobs, but on developing skills. It is skills that are the new currency. Roles have changed and the way that results are achieved may be very different to how they were before. Often leaders don't really understand what their employees do on a day-to-day basis, in fact in OC Tanner's 2021 *Global Culture Report* only 59% of employees said that their leaders know what they do. Digital transformation is agile and ongoing, and the workforce needs to adapt their thinking and learn new skills in real-time as they meet new challenges. Furthermore, work itself is more distributed. People work across teams, functions and disciplines, sometimes on projects over which their line manager has no visibility. Performance is much more multi-faceted and linked to recognition. Engagement is something that ebbs and flows in real-time depending, as we saw in the previous chapter, much more on the daily interactions between employees, teams, technology, clients and customers, as it does on interventions by the business.

As a result of these changes, traditional talent management needs an overhaul. Digital talent has intellectual curiosity, a desire to discover and understand how their roles are evolving. They look for support, enablement, connections, self-management and access to what they need to know as and when they need it. The key to ensuring this happens is through culture. The business needs a culture of learning, a culture of performance, a culture of recognition and appreciation, all leading to a culture of innovation.

Embracing remote and flexible working

Before exploring the specific ways in which talent management is evolving, we first need to consider how it is impacted by the way our workplaces themselves are currently changing, and the wider impacts it has. During 2020/21 we saw a huge increase in flexible and remote working become a reality for many global employees, although not in a way they had ever imagined. In response to the COVID-19 pandemic, offices needed to close, or at best keep only skeleton staffing, while several of the roles in the technology, business and professional service sectors became remote. For many, this shift to remote working meant employees taking a more flexible approach, balancing their job responsibilities with family concerns, such as home-schooling children or shielding vulnerable parents and relatives. For many years the research has indicated that the opportunity to work remotely and/or flexibly is a key benefit for employees and job seekers. In their 2019 International Employee Survey, WorkHuman found by some distance that the opportunity to work remotely or flexibly was the most important workplace perk. Meanwhile, in our 2018 research among 14,000 jobseekers, we found 61% agreeing that the opportunity to have flexible working hours was important when deciding where to work, making it more important than locational flexibility. However, over half (55%) told us that what they really wanted was a combination of both office and home working. Only 31% preferred to be in an office full time. One of the most telling findings in our 2018 survey was that 84% believed that the jobs they were applying for could be done from home with the right support. When asked about the roles they were currently doing, the majority did not have the option to work from home, although nearly three-quarters (71%) believed they had the tools and technology to do so productively. Only one in five said their current employer actively encouraged working from home, with just a quarter believing their corporate culture supported it. Supporting their employees to work flexibly has been – and remains as we write this book – a major leadership challenge. However, organizations should also be mindful of the fact that two of the largest problems remote working can create are a loss of connection and a feeling of isolation. Our 2018 research found only 34% saying that they never felt isolated while working from home. Over two-thirds of our respondents said that the benefit of being in an office was to have easier interactions with colleagues, with around half saying the social aspects of being around colleagues was important to them in their work. During 2020/21 we saw managers of remote teams working hard to address this with interventions such as open information sharing and encouraging their teams to do likewise, setting expectations but showing that they trust their teams by focusing on outcomes as opposed to activity, and maintaining continuity by scheduling regular one-to-one and team meetings. Working remotely isn't a panacea for everyone though. Research from organizational consultancy Leesman found that in the UK only 41% of homeworkers had a dedicated room or office. Digging a little deeper it transpired that 72% of under-25s do not have a dedicated room to work in at home and struggle to connect with colleagues. This effectively leaves younger workers without the resources to own a property, working in their bedrooms, and later going to sleep in their offices. This also impacts the informal learning opportunities that many younger employees previously gained from meetings and conversations (direct or overheard) with more experienced colleagues. These would help their advancement and provide much needed 'ground truth' in understanding how their organization really operated, and insight into the opportunities for advancement. A deficiency of this 'social capital' can hold back career development.

Most contact happens through video calls, which bring their own problems. According to an interview with Gianpiero Petriglieri, an associate professor at INSEAD, being on a video call requires more focus than a face-to-face conversation. This is because we must work harder processing non–verbal cues – such as facial expressions, body language and the pitch and tone of voices – which consumes more energy and doesn't allow us to feel relaxed about the conversation. Silence was identified as another problem. In a real-life conversation, it can set a rhythm and flow, but over a video call, it creates anxiety. A 2014 study from Germany found that delays on phone or conferencing systems shaped a negative view of the people we were speaking to, while a delay of even two seconds can lead to us gaining a negative perception of the speaker. Video calls also remind us of the people we have temporarily lost social contact with, mainly the colleagues with whom we are usually sharing the workplace. As we shall see in a later section, they are also not very effective for remote performance management. In a recent research project, we found the majority of managers having difficulty using video technology effectively for remote performance management, with ad-hoc catch-ups, and more difficult performance-related conversations, proving particularly difficult. When looking at conversations between employees, data from the WorkHuman recognition platforms show that in the early days of the COVID-19 pandemic, the most used words in digital interactions were 'continuity', 'flexibility', 'resilience' and 'adversity'. These are all words indicating a challenge. However, as things progressed, and employees became more settled in their new working environments, these words changed to 'friend', 'kindness', 'connectivity' and 'compassion'. This showed a more human and supportive side as people began to settle in their new working reality. When WorkHuman then surveyed 500 full-time employees in the US in September 2020 to get a better understanding of the role employee recognition had played during COVID-19, they found almost half (49.4%) saying that they had never received a 'thank you' from either their colleagues or their manager during the pandemic at that point. This was a huge, missed opportunity to help build human connections during a time of stress and uncertainty, and address any fears or stress that employees may have had.

We will look at the important role recognition and giving thanks plays in creating a thriving, inclusive culture later in the book. At this stage, suffice to say, it takes on greater importance at times of uncertainty and disruption.

Creating a culture of learning

Towards the end of 2018, we surveyed a group of around 500 UK employees (across sectors and functions) and an exclusive group of senior UK HR and learning and development professionals to find out more about attitudes to learning. We had already been involved with a survey of 14,000 job seekers, one of the findings being that the main thing they were looking for from a new employer was the opportunity to learn and develop new skills. Some of our findings have already been referenced but there were several key things that we found. First, that with the quickening pace of digital transformation employers need to be able to access and retain talent with the right skills at the right time and that 70% of the employees said that opportunities for learning were essential when looking where to work, and for 98% it was crucial when deciding whether to stay. One of the more surprising themes was that over 60% wanted to take control over how and when they learn, and only one out of six wanted to learn at times arranged by their employer. While the majority of the remaining five out of six expected to learn during work hours, they wanted it to be under their own direction. In other words, they want access to information and knowledge at the time when they find that they need it. One person we interviewed summed up the view of many in saying they wanted to learn and be able to apply that learning to real scenarios at work. If you think of the modern digital world, this makes sense. The way we consume information has changed. I'm sure most readers have tried to assemble a flat-pack cupboard or bed or tried their hand at gardening or car maintenance. How do we find out what we need to know? Search online and probably check videos in which a range of people, from skilled craftsmen to weekend hobbyists, explain how to do it. It is only natural for this to transfer to the workplace, where employers will need to provide similar access. For a long time, employers have thought of learning as something that happens in a classroom, using content designed by an instructor, and that this is the best way to ensure the skills and knowledge of their people remain current, and performance is improved. While most of these courses have always been well designed and delivered, they are no longer relevant to a work environment in which our people need to be more agile and innovative in both their thinking and the way they approach their work. The core principle at the heart of this development is the shift from a culture of training to a culture of learning, with an organization's competitive advantage being its collective knowledge and expertise. This means moving away from an instructor-led, centralized and event-based approach to training, and embracing a learner-orientated, continuous, decentralized and shared experience approach of learning, with success being measured by results and not course completion. In their April 2020 report *Creating Learning Cultures: Assessing The Evidence*[3] the CIPD describes a learning culture as one that 'embeds learning into how things are done at an individual, team and organizational level' requiring leaders to 'support employees towards a collectively shared vision and positive change through open dialogue and reflection'. Their research showed that while 98% of learning and development practitioners wanted to develop a positive culture for learning, only 36% felt that this had been achieved.

The main barriers to embedding a learning culture that their research identified were:

- A tendency to confuse learning with formal training and knowledge management.
- An approach that tried to structure informal learning leaving employees lacking agency in and ownership of their own learning needs.
- Lack of support or buy-in from senior leaders and line managers.
- Siloed approaches across more complex and multi-function businesses.

A key recommendation from the research was the reframing of 'learning culture' as 'learning environment' – negating the impact of senior leaders who are in a position to mould overall 'culture' within an organization. They believe that 'environment' is an easier concept for individual learning professionals to implement, although still a key element in the overall learning culture. One of the core behaviours they identified that learning professionals need to develop when trying to create an overall learning culture is professional courage and influence, the ability to speak up and share their vision even when resistance or opposition are expected. This requires people to develop effective communication skills that can challenge more orthodox approaches, while making the case for new and emerging approaches that will improve knowledge and performance.

Digital talent should be hired for and rewarded for their intellectual curiosity and thrive in an environment that can nurture critical thinking. They favour constructive and meaningful feedback and are unlikely to respond to managers who duck out of having difficult conversations. And they respond to leaders who are constantly learning and developing themselves too.

Learning during a time of hybrid and remote working

We have already established that learning is something that happens on an ongoing basis, in real-time, and not at specific times set by an organization. For this to happen successfully our workers need access to tools and knowledge whenever and wherever they are working, something which modern learning technology platforms enable. Their effectiveness was put to the test during 2020 and 2021 as large numbers had to start using these tools remotely.

As part of a major research project during the summer of 2020, we surveyed and interviewed several organizations. For the vast majority, their number one priority was employee development, keeping their people relevant and capable of adapting to changing circumstances, by giving them access to the learning they needed. Development through digital learning was seen as key across the whole organization, not just for selected employee groups. While almost three-quarters identified that there was an increased demand for digital learning from their people, only just over a quarter of the businesses we surveyed felt that their technology had given their people the access they needed. The largest cohort (almost 40%) believed that while their employees got access to the learning they needed, there were some problems, and a third identified that their people had significant problems getting access to the information they needed.

One area in which we noticed the need for an improvement was in providing peer-to-peer connection and interaction. Global HR analyst Josh Bersin often talks of how 'people need more contact, not more content'. He stresses the importance of complementing online learning with peer-to-peer interaction and collaboration.

Over the last couple of years, the increased use of video conferencing to replicate business meetings may give the impression of improving connection, however, workplace learning has often been done in isolation. Video meetings bring their own problems, something we shall cover in more detail when we talk about performance management, however the opportunity to help promote shared learning experiences is one area that businesses should experiment with.

One concern that we have is that while almost all the organizations we spoke to admitted that they want their technology to provide a great user experience to their people, the reality is that this doesn't always happen. Throughout the research project, we identified employees who felt they weren't getting access to the knowledge they needed at the times they most wanted it. While HR and learning leaders believed they were putting the needs of their people first, making user experience one of the key considerations when investing in technology, barely one in five said that they involved employees in the decision-making process, with almost half (45%) admitting that despite getting employee input, the final investment decision was made elsewhere, by a combination of finance, IT teams and senior leadership. In fact, a third of the companies surveyed admitted that employees were rarely ever consulted.

The user experience of workplace technology has become a key factor in both employee engagement and their overall satisfaction levels. In an area such as virtual learning, where we need to help our people with regular upskilling and to increase their knowledge base, it is crucial. We would urge all organizations to try and find a way of involving the employee user experience in their decision-making processes around technology investments.

The rise of talent intelligence

In the last chapter, we explored how the filling of new roles had gradually shifted away from internal promotion and lateral assignments to external hiring over the last 20 years or so. In the modern complex, multi-capability organization it is not always possible for a hiring manager or talent acquisition specialist to know what skills, capabilities and knowledge are available within the business. With people sometimes working cross-project, cross-function and even cross-location, their own manager may not always be aware of what they are working on.

We have already referenced the statistic that up to two-thirds of employees say it is easier to find a new role in a different business than it is to move within their own. During 2020/2021 there was a shift in focus towards utilizing the skills and knowledge that already exist within a business, and it would be wrong to attribute this wholly to changes in approaches to recruitment bought about by the COVID-19 pandemic. The truth is that most forward-thinking organizations were already looking at ways in which to move their people around. Internal talent mobility has been an issue that has been getting more priority on the HR agenda in recent years, although it has taken time to secure its place. In our previous book, *Exceptional Talent,* we explored how the reluctance of line managers to lose their best performers had led to a more siloed approach to filling new roles, leading to an external-first focus, while at the same time people were leaving organizations because of a lack of opportunity to grow, develop and learn new skills. One of the reasons that this trend continued to grow was through a lack of data and insight on existing employees in a place that was accessible to everyone within an organization. There also seemed little interest in tracking how employees developed once they left, even from those businesses with good alumni networks, or even analysing the backgrounds of those who had become top performers after joining. When searching for people with skills and knowledge of technology, neither of which may have existed a few short years ago, gut instinct or general feelings about an interviewee are not enough. The modern organization needs precise, compelling data to support hiring decisions, which has led to increased investment in the area of talent intelligence. For several years we have seen the importance of people analytics grow within organizations as technology helps us find ways to collect and analyse data, whether it is about performance, learning or recruitment. People analytics can tend to be quite inwardly-focused, relying on the internal tools and data, whereas talent intelligence is different in that it uses a mix of internal and external data and market information. Talent intelligence can focus on many strands of data and information, starting with employment history (which can also include salary and education history). We can analyse the skills which an employee has, supplemented with data on recently learned skills from our learning management system, performance data collected from previous performance reviews, as well as salary and benefits information. Some systems may look to include available insights from previous conversations with line managers and senior leaders and in some cases even a social media history. Data will exist on those currently in talent pools or candidate pipelines, as well as those working for competitors who may have previously shown an interest in working for our organization but have not followed through on an application. There may also be broader data on people working within the sector, highlighting those who may have a specific passion for the sector and possess relevant skills.

Many businesses use publicly available labour market analysis to help build skills roadmaps. Current employee data can then be compared to highlight roles where skills are already possessed within the organization and other areas where skills might be lacking, therefore requiring either some specific or targeted hiring, or else identifying areas for internal skill development. A broader skills roadmap can be built moving forward. Some organizations can use talent intelligence to identify sources of potential performance differentials between internal teams and teams who may be working for competitors. This enables them to measure expected performance and identify any output boost that could result from increasing the training for employees in skills that have become essential to roles within a specific industry sector. Ultimately these data and analysis should be used to understand what is changing internally and externally and to predict what may happen in the external talent market, making the insights most valuable when blended with internal data.

The HR Trends Institute listed 'From job-based HR to skills-based HR' as one of its 2021 megatrends. The ability to know and understand the current skills, the skills that can be acquired and the adjacent skills (those related to a skill or competency that a worker already has) will be hugely important in the future.

Using talent intelligence

Organizations that are proficient at generating and analysing data will be using talent intelligence to make better people decisions. This isn't always about hiring though. Research from a variety of sources shows the key metrics organizations use this data for include:

- quality of hire;
- employee engagement;
- critical business roles for which no successor has been identified;
- competency or skills gap analysis;
- average time to hire for key roles;
- best sources of hire;
- top performer retention.

This indicates the importance of talent acquisition, HR and the learning and development teams working closely together, sharing data and insights. When organizations struggle to create this environment, it is usually through either a lack of internal analytics capability, investing in the wrong tools or a lack of support from senior management teams.

There is currently huge investment from the HR technology sector into creating market-leading talent intelligence platforms. As interest in this area grows it is worth considering what a successful platform should include. One area in which organizations will often differ from each other is in creating skill taxonomies – the integration and categorization of skills and capabilities. Because most jobs can be quite complex once undertaken, many organizations may end up with sets of complex and wide-ranging competencies for different roles. Using AI, a true talent intelligence platform should allow companies to source, identify and intelligently move people around with a deep reservoir of knowledge. As leading HR analyst Josh Bersin says, 'business capabilities are made up of skills, relationships, and experiences – all of which must be reflected in the platform'. AI will also allow platforms to quickly 'learn' how to optimize and personalize intelligence to fit specific business and recruiting needs.

In his 2020 paper *The Rise of The Talent Intelligence Platform* Bersin expands on his ideas of matching people to opportunities in a more accurate way. He gives the example of hiring a marketing manager.[4] Most recruitment systems are created to help you identify someone who already has that role, whether they are inside or outside your organization. However, what happens if the role is newly created? Or is intended to be a development opportunity for someone? Perhaps it is time to find someone who can take a completely different approach to the role?

A talent intelligence platform should help with this, by identifying adjacent skills, people who may be known to the organization, companies an individual has worked for, time spent in various jobs, education, and work locations. Basically, the platform should provide a much richer and more insightful view of potential individuals. The advice Bersin gave to get started was to simplify the job architecture (by simplifying and broadening job descriptions), define the skills you really need in each role, and to start small and expand incrementally.

Embracing internal mobility

One of the main problems that arise when internal routes for employee progression are limited is that precious time and budget are diverted away from employee development, instead being allocated to finding and assessing experienced people working elsewhere. For many businesses, the default position to filling roles is to look externally. In autumn 2020 we partnered with performance and talent management software company Actus to research how organizations were approaching internal mobility. One of our key findings was that only 5% of the businesses we surveyed looked internally first when trying to fill new positions. We shall explore some of the reasons during this section, however, we did notice a slight shift in this approach emerging as the COVID-19 pandemic led to some organizations imposing external hiring freezes. One of the key reasons why internal employees were being overlooked was the reluctance of business leaders to look internally, with only one in five organizations we spoke to saying that internal mobility was important to their leaders. The main reason given for this was that leaders often feel they need a broader mix of skills, experience and perspectives that can only come from greater external hiring. The counterpoint to this approach was that almost two-thirds (62%) admitted that employees leave their businesses to take on roles that could have been offered to them internally, had they known about them or been considered. The factors we uncovered were cultural and technological. Many managers admitted that they want to hold on to their best performers so prefer not to have their performance data visible, leaving this data either existing in silos or going unrecorded and being purely anecdotal. A lack of meaningful performance-related data was a common complaint, with many of the managers we interviewed feeling that the blame lay with HR for allowing this to develop, while HR leaders themselves felt that attitudes would only change when their HR technology was upgraded.

The key obstacles to redeploying internal talent that we uncovered were:

- Leaders not having a full understanding of all the capabilities in their teams.
- Line managers not wanting to lose skills and knowledge from their teams.
- Lack of visibility of skills data.
- Managers wanting people who can be productive immediately (i.e. have done the role before).
- Directors thinking that it is fairer to appoint externally than to be seen as selecting individuals for progression.

The overriding view was that internal mobility only happened when it was employee-led. However, this situation has developed primarily because senior leaders have failed to prioritize employee development through mobility which, in turn, has led to a culture of external hiring, and the siloing of performance, skill and capability data. This cycle needs to be broken, and from our research, it looks like things are beginning to change. Talent management is becoming more of a business and HR imperative, with internal mobility itself coming more under the remit of talent acquisition, when it comes to filling newly created roles.

Talent intelligence platforms combine data from multiple internal and external sources, which helps with increased transparency of skills, people and performance in the business, identifying the employees who are ready to take on new challenges. It is also clear that visibility of internal opportunities to develop and grow within their organization positively impacts employee engagement, thereby further improving retention and advocacy. When candidates apply, they want to know that you are a place where they can grow, so contented employees, and alumni, will always be the best advocates for your approaches to talent management and internal mobility.

From performance management to performance enablement

If we are to support and enable our people to learn, grow and develop the skills and capabilities that the business needs then the way we support their performance needs to reflect this.

In our previous book, *Exceptional Talent*, we wrote about how performance management had transitioned from a periodic process of rating, ranking and reviewing employees, not unlike an end of term school report, into something more inclusive and supportive in which managers had ongoing conversations with their people. It can effectively be viewed as shifting the approach from periodic review to continuous development. In fact, the move away from periodic reviews, and also forced rankings, towards offering ongoing support effectively began around 2015/2016 when a number of high-profile corporates rejected the more traditional approach that had become known as 'rank and yank' after being championed by the General Electric CEO Jack Welch in the latter part of the 20th century.[5] The CIPD, reporting in 2016,[6] said that there was 'good evidence' to ditch forced rankings given that most employees saw them as both arbitrary and unfair, and most importantly, believed that it did not show a true reflection of their actual performance or the value of the work they had done. The modern approach to managing performance is that while ratings alone can't improve employees, relationships do. It follows that there are two important principles managers have to embrace to complete this transition. First, there is a mindset change from 'how do I manage and rank your performance' to 'how can I support and enable you to do your best and to achieve your full potential'. And second, there is the recognition that performance isn't something that happens each month, quarter or year, but something that happens every day. Inclusive and effective performance management should be firmly at the very heart of management and leadership culture. Shifting from appraisals to conversations means changing from one-way reporting to two-way feedback and conversation, and mindsets go from managing performance to enabling and supporting people. It is often said of managers that if they are not developing their people then they are holding them back. Embracing this approach requires more than a tweak in management style. It needs a total change in culture, strategy, rewards and embracing a different mindset. Ratings do not improve an employee's performance, but relationships will.

The journey is complicated, and for a lot of businesses, it is not yet fully happening. But progress is being made. Research from US analysts Brandon Hall Group[7] found that 54% of organizations use frequent performance conversations and coaching to supplement their annual performance appraisals, with 44% also using appraisals to focus more on future goals and expectations, rather than to review past performance. However, anecdotally, when most companies were asked how often they have performance conversations, many admitted that they only happen periodically – usually half-yearly or annually. Only around one in six are having conversations on an ongoing basis, mostly taking the form of regular catch-ups on a monthly basis between managers and employees. One interesting finding from this research was that only around one in seven companies has managed to completely eliminate rankings and formal appraisals but that this, in part, was down to the employees themselves wanting to know where they stand in comparison to their peers and how they were performing against their manager's expectations. It's important to make the distinction here between ratings that can enable employees to benchmark their improvement and performance scores that seem final and can be demotivating. Using modern people analytics, managers should have a rich dataset that measures all employee inputs and achievements that can help to properly assess performance, potential and impact. This shows why, for many businesses, performance management is still rooted in the manager-employee relationship. Historically, this has been a fairly linear relationship, following the pattern of an organizational chart. However, as we've already discussed, modern businesses are no longer hierarchical and tend to work differently. In fact, managers might not be aware of how the employees they are responsible for are performing as they could be working across teams, functions, divisions or even borders. And if they are working on a series of projects, recognition can come from anywhere across various teams, functions or divisions, and can come from anyone responsible for them irrespective of their employment status (e.g. freelance or contract workers).

In this book, as in our previous one, we point to the problem that most managers are rewarded for having high performing teams rather than for developing them. As we have already seen, this causes problems for internal mobility, with managers wanting to keep their best performers, but it also creates problems for, and entrenches approaches to, performance management. Most managers tend to focus on the development and direction of their perceived best performers at the expense of helping those who may be most in need of help. We have already said that if managers are not developing their people, then they are holding them back, and this applies to all members of their teams irrespective of their potential and previous achievements. To build the best and most supportive relationships with their people, managers need to properly understand each individual's strengths and capabilities within that team, what motivates them and how best to encourage them.

Since early 2020, most performance management has been conducted remotely. During the summer 2020 research we referenced earlier, we also surveyed companies to see how they were adapting to remote performance management. Only 28%, just over one in four, responded positively with the rest admitting some, or many, difficulties for both managers and their employees. The parts that adapted most successfully were the more specific actions, such as goal setting and the recording of formal feedback. However, it was in the more informal parts of the process, particularly those involving ad-hoc chats and feedback, and difficult performance-related conversations, that organizations and their employees reported problems. There were understandably also problems with what some respondents called 'observational management' when it came to assessing performance. As we described in an earlier section in this chapter, video conferencing is not satisfactory for these types of difficult one-to-one conversations. This is especially true for performance management as the ability to gauge the reactions of an employee, to tell how the feedback has landed, makes it hard to offer the appropriate level and type of support.

The problem with feedback and how to fix it

Shifting from performance management to performance enablement puts greater focus on the words you use when giving feedback. Their meaning is hugely important during one-to-one reviews. Unfortunately, feedback has a bit of an image problem. The word itself conjures up the vision of something offered but not asked for, and possibly something that the recipient will not like. Our brains are not always ready to hear it, particularly if it is delivered at an unscheduled time, and the words used can often be open to interpretation and misinterpretation. Especially if the conversations are happening over video conferencing. We need feedback to be supportive, however, the role it has historically played in performance management has often been negative. Individuals will automatically latch on to any negative connotations, so words are important. The wrong words, or the incorrect context, can hurt, give offence or demotivate. Receiving recognition and feedback should be a positive experience for our people. One that enables them to grow and develop as individuals and employees, but managers can still make it negative through their language and framing. Part of their own development as people leaders needs to ensure that they are able to make feedback informative, positive and supportive.

As we mentioned in the opening chapter, while speaking at the WorkHuman conference in 2019, Kat Cole[8] (COO of Focus Brands North America) talked of how her job as a leader wasn't to keep everyone happy but was to help everyone to do their best work. She said that leaders would be failing their people if they didn't make that happen. For this approach to succeed it needs businesses to have a culture of giving constructive, helpful and enabling feedback, something which starts at the very top of the organization and sets the tone for management at all levels. In fact, Tamra Chandler,[9] a US CEO who has authored two books on performance management and feedback, says that by concentrating on the strengths of your people across the whole organization, feedback will determine how you are seen as a leader. Summarizing her writing, we can identify three main problems with feedback:

· Too many leaders and managers have a misguided belief that it requires 'brutal honesty'.
· It has become something that is 'dumped' on us at various times of the year rather than something that is used constructively when needed.
· As individuals we tend to turn it back on to the giver, spiralling the negativity.

Research indicates that development-orientated feedback is a key driver in engagement and in creating feelings of inclusion. It can give employees a belief that what they do is important and that their manager or leader can see something positive in them that they may not have seen themselves. We know that positive feedback creates feelings of energy and enthusiasm in individuals and can help them feel trusted and respected. On the contrary, anecdotal evidence tends to indicate that negative feedback leaves people feeling isolated and has them focusing more energy on anything with a negative connotation, even if there are positives in what they hear or read.

So, can we fix feedback?

In her book, Tamra Chandler writes that managers and leaders need to completely change the way they see feedback. They need to use it as a way to help people, to look to the future and help them move forward. Unhelpful or negative feedback doesn't support people in that way. The best feedback, that really works for employees, is fair and focused and delivered regularly. The best way to deliver feedback is through a two-way conversation between a manager or leader and their employee, rather than a one-way judgement with no discussion, which can often lead to a breakdown in trust and the employee/manager relationship becoming defensive. For this reason, it is best if feedback is based on behaviours and actions that have been observed and noticed, rather than passed on anecdotally. On this point, it is worth noting what Kat Cole said in the presentation we quoted earlier 'Instead of assuming that a failure or mistake on the part of an employee is his or her fault, ask yourself if there is something in your business or structure that caused it'. As with performance management, feedback is as much to do with the culture of the organization as the personality of managers and leaders. Tamra Chandler identifies three personas in the feedback cycle, and I think they can be used in all organizations. First, there are what she calls 'seekers'. These are the people within your organization who seek out feedback as they look to improve, and they tend to have a clear idea of the type of feedback they need, how they want to hear it and how they will act upon it. The second persona is 'receivers'. These are the employees who are more passive. They hear the feedback but are more likely to become defensive and to focus on any negative interpretation about what they hear. The final persona is 'extenders'. These are the managers and leaders who really notice what their people are doing, and they ground their conclusions and feedback in observations and facts. Extenders also tend to be clear on the purpose of their feedback and sensitive to the timing and framing of its delivery.

Unsurprisingly, the advice for improving the way feedback can support development is to create an organization of seekers and extenders. Most readers will probably identify a number of receivers in their organizations, but these can skillfully be converted into seekers through the right organizational culture. We shall be looking more closely at leadership in the next chapter, however when it comes to creating the right culture for supportive and enabling feedback, it requires honest, brave leaders who can set the tone in which a culture of recognition and respect can thrive.

Why onboarding is so important for successful talent management

All of the talent management interventions we have written about in this chapter should support and enable our people to achieve their full potential and help them to become productive and engaged employees. We saw in the previous chapter the importance of both micro experiences and sentiment in determining whether a job candidate accepts an offer, and how at key times during the interview, hiring and offer phases of their journey they feel that there is a lack of information. We used the analogy of a relay race to describe the talent lifecycle and how after an offer is accepted many organizations effectively 'drop the baton' when it comes to onboarding. We can't stress strongly enough how important the process of onboarding is. It is the way we transition a new employee from the application journey to becoming the settled, productive and engaged employee we need. While there might be confusion within some organizations as to who should take responsibility for onboarding (hence the dropped baton analogy) we believe that it is actually everyone's responsibility – talent acquisition, IT, HR, learning and development, the hiring manager, the line manager senior leaders and their colleagues. Onboarding should start early. The process before an offer is accepted is usually known as pre-boarding. As soon as we move to the second interview stage the likelihood is that one of the interviewees will be our new employee. We also know that we have a group of candidates who could be good enough to join us and who might therefore become an employee when we hire at some stage in the future. In other words, those who don't get an offer this time might well be open to receiving an offer in the future, so the experience they get is of paramount importance. They can be advocates and ambassadors of the type of company we are to work for, which starts with how we treat people during hiring.

We've previously mentioned that employees sometimes decide quite early in their employment to leave an organization, particularly if they are not happy with the way they are settling in or they believe in their first few months that they have made a mistake. This will often happen when they don't feel the job is what they expected, or they struggle to build rapport or relationships with their team and/or their manager. So, it's crucial that a new hire feels part of the organization as soon as they join, if not sooner. It's often said that they need to feel part of the business before they have even switched on their computer. Early onboarding helps to address the possibility that a new hire can sometimes feel overwhelmed or disengaged during the first weeks of an employment relationship. Most new hires say that quality one-to-one time spent with their manager is the most important part of their first few days and months. New hires also need supportive colleagues and wider networks to help show them around, offer advice and guidance, and pass on some of the ground truth knowledge of how the organization operates. Giving them opportunities to connect to the rest of their team, and other key colleagues, before joining will help to build the relationships they need, as well as acquainting them with the cultural norms associated with their team or division. By starting early, we also address the possibility that they could become overwhelmed and disengaged early in the employment relationship. They should already be familiar with their duties, responsibilities and objectives. They will also need to understand the expectations of their performance and achievements over the first few weeks and months, plus have visibility of clear reporting lines. In fact, research from Glassdoor found that organizations with strong onboarding processes improve new hire retention by 82%.[10]

We can summarize the four key components of successful onboarding as:

- Starting the process early.
- Helping the new employee to establish personal connections.
- Ensuring they have clear objectives, goals and timelines, with a structure for feedback so there are no surprises.
- Making the first day as special as possible.

It should also be remembered that onboarding isn't just for employees new to the business. Earlier in this chapter, we looked at how internal mobility was being increasingly used by organizations to cover skills gaps and to retain knowledge and capability within the business. Internal hires need onboarding too, through a process normally referred to as cross-boarding. It cannot be assumed that someone moving within an organization will know all the formalities, expectations, cultural norms and objectives in other teams, sections, divisions or functions of the business. Onboarding platforms should be used for these types of moves too.

Chapter summary

The business of tomorrow will not be based around creating jobs, but on developing skills; there will be a shift from job-based HR to skills-based HR. A 'culture of learning' needs to embed learning into how things are done at an individual, team and organizational level, which requires leaders to support employees towards a collectively shared vision and positive change through open dialogue and reflection. In this chapter, we have seen:

- Employees need more contact and connection, not just more learning content. It is important to complement online learning with peer-to-peer interaction, discussion and collaboration.
- Having robust and comprehensive talent intelligence data and analytics is key to understanding the capabilities and skills that exist in the business, and to help maximize productivity and performance.

- Internal mobility is now a business imperative as a way of ensuring that necessary skills and knowledge are retained in the business. Too many employees leave to take roles they could have performed internally.

- Performance management has to be used to support and enable employees to be able to do their best work and to achieve their full potential.

- Early and comprehensive onboarding is the key to successful talent management and talent development.

Endnotes

1 World Economic Forum. The Future of Jobs Report 2020, www.weforum.org/reports/the-future-of-jobs-report-2020 (archived at https://perma.cc/72ZE-W9FX)

2 P Petrone. The Skills Companies Need Most in 2018 – And The Courses to Get Them, LinkedIn, 2 January 2018. www.linkedin.com/business/learning/blog/top-skills-and-courses/the-skills-companies-need-most-in-2018-and-the-courses-to-get (archived at https://perma.cc/RH9W-3KWC)

3 CIPD. Creating Learning Cultures Report, April 2020. www.cipd.co.uk/Images/creating-learning-cultures-1_tcm18-75606.pdf (archived at https://perma.cc/8PPB-4CML)

4 J Bersin. The Rise of the Talent Intelligence Platform, media.trustradius.com/product-downloadables/V0/W0/WJDDJTF4GJ44.pdf (archived at https://perma.cc/89W7-6Z8N)

5 J Faragher. Performance: Why 'rank and yank' fell out of favour, *Personnel Today*, 26 February 2021. www.personneltoday.com/hr/why-rank-and-yank-fell-out-of-favour/ (archived at https://perma.cc/X3SG-YUPH)

6 CIPD. Could do better? Assessing what works in performance management, cipd.co.uk/knowledge/fundamentals/people/performance/what-works-in-performance-management-report (archived at https://perma.cc/4KC5-AW9B)

7 D Forry. 5 Essential Performance Management Strategies, Brandon Hall Group, 23 October 2018. www.brandonhall.com/blogs/5-essential-performance-management-strategies/ (archived at https://perma.cc/7A2M-VVDD)

8 WorkHuman. Globoforce Announces Business Executive Kat Cole as Keynote Speaker for WorkHuman 2019 Conference, 16 October 2018. www.workhuman.com/press-releases/kat-cole-workhuman-2019/ (archived at https://perma.cc/AB6Q-6P2S)

9 T Chandler. www.tamrachandler.com/ (archived at https://perma.cc/U3SA-NLTM)

10 J Dewar. 10 Employee Onboarding Statistics you Must Know in 2021, Sapling HR, 5 October 2021. www.saplinghr.com/10-employee-onboarding-statistics-you-must-know-in-2021 (archived at https://perma.cc/7GNS-4PA8)

05

Leadership in the digital age

In the August 2013 edition of *Harvard Business Review* the former CEO of HCL Technologies, Vineet Nayar,[1] wrote about the differences between managers and leaders. He said: 'Management consists of controlling a group or a set of entities to accomplish a goal. Leadership refers to an individual's ability to influence, motivate, and enable others to contribute toward organizational success'. His point was that leadership is defined by influence and inspiration while management can often be about power and control. He further talked of how leadership focuses on creating and generating value, while management was usually more concerned with counting value.

We are used to seeing businesses become defined by who leads them. From Henry Ford to modern-day digital creators such as Bill Gates, Steve Jobs, Jeff Bezos or Mark Zuckerberg, we tend to personalize leadership and project our own preferred characteristics onto them. We don't think of modern leaders as managers but as visionaries, who are able to influence the way we live and motivate their workforce to share their visions.

The events of 2020/21, as the world at large grappled with the ramifications of the COVID-19 pandemic, has put leadership firmly in the spotlight and it appears that it is business leaders who people have been looking towards for guidance. The 2021 Edelman Trust Barometer[2] found that private business is the most trusted institution globally, having moved far ahead of governments and NGOs. An overwhelming 86% said they expected CEOs and business leaders to take the lead on social issues, with just over three-quarters (68%)

also saying that CEOs should step in when governments cannot fix societal problems. While the public at large may be looking towards business leaders, within organizations the reality seems slightly more nuanced. In their 2021 *Global Culture Report*, O.C. Tanner[3] found just over a third of UK workers saying they had lost confidence in their senior leadership since the start of the COVID-19 pandemic. This was illustrated by almost 40% feeling unsupported by their senior leaders, with a similar proportion saying they felt isolated and vulnerable within their jobs. Despite this, both PWC[4] and Deloitte[5] found in their recent CEO surveys that leaders' concerns are about building public trust and focusing on their people. Business growth, technological developments, digital transformation and cybersecurity were also raised as important issues. Leaders know that they often need to use their voices to speak out about the societal issues that impact their people. Around 80% say they will choose to speak out on issues that align with their organization's strategic purpose and values, while a third also take into account their own personal values and conscience.

Recent years have seen increasing opportunities for business leaders to use their voices. A focus on overhauling their approaches to diversity, equality and inclusion following the murder of George Floyd in the US and the growth of the Black Lives Matter campaign is an obvious recent example. Taking a much more proactive approach to addressing their employees' physical and mental wellbeing, particularly in the wake of the COVID-19 pandemic, is another priority, even though the O.C. Tanner research we referenced earlier may indicate there is still a way to go. In reality, these very public events are built on an already existing prioritization of improvement within most major organizations. Employee feedback, increasingly gathered through employee recognition and experience software and the conversational AI that underpins them, has shown concern over how organizations tackle much broader issues.

This is of particular importance to the younger, emerging workforce that we have recruited and integrated within businesses over the last few years and will continue to do across the next few years as well. They are proving to be one of the most diverse groups of workers, with a keen interest in environmental, social and governance issues, and a belief that their employers should commit to improving their performance in areas affecting diversity, equality and inclusion, as well as sustainability and climate change. While it is often said that younger employees look for purpose in their work, the reality is that they also look for purpose in how their employers address emerging global issues. And they don't mind making their voices heard, as we will see later in this chapter.

A sudden escalation of public trust, possibly driven by the uncertainty surrounding the COVID-19 pandemic, has given business leaders a once in a generation opportunity to rethink their legacy and purpose, and to take the lead on justice, inclusion and global well-being. As Latha Poonamallee,[6] author of *Expansive Leadership: Cultivating Mindfulness to Lead Self and Others in a Changing World,* wrote in June 2021: 'Leadership is about stepping up, showing up, and trying to do the right thing when the opportunity presents itself. Now is a great window of opportunity for leaders at all levels to exercise their immense power for good and be champions of justice'.

What makes great leadership for our people?

The role that leaders play in shaping the culture, values and purpose of an organization makes them a major contributor to the employee experience. Furthermore, their actions influence the type of business you are to work for. In the survey of 14,000 European jobseekers that we conducted a couple of years ago, just over 83% said that strong leadership was an important factor in whether they were successful in their role. The two most important factors they gave that would support their success – having a collaborative working environment and being in a business with a clear vision and values – both depend heavily on having great leaders. So, what are the qualities that our employees feel define great leadership? For just over half of our respondents, it was accountability and honesty. The two can often be linked. US author and TED speaker Brene Brown often talks of accountability being necessary for leaders because 'The opposite of accountability is [to] blame. Accountability is a vulnerable process that takes courage and time. Blame is faster'. For jobseekers, it is this mix of taking responsibility and ownership that seems important in their leaders. Honesty is also important in building trust between leaders and their people. A more trusting environment also leads to a happier and more productive workforce, as the truth can help them to identify, and help address, any business issues. The next two most important qualities are decisiveness and confidence. It is clearly interesting that these do not rank as important as the more vulnerable, and some might say human, characteristics of accountability and honesty. This could reflect a younger demographic who look for leaders who take a more caring and purposeful approach. Popular culture often portrays business leaders as more autocratic hirers and firers, whereas employees look for softer and more personal approaches, something evidenced by our survey respondents highlighting awareness and empathy as the next most important qualities. In an era of uncertainty for business in general, it maybe wasn't a surprise to see that optimism and focus are the least important qualities for great leadership.

Interestingly for those in multi-national organizations, we found that across Europe the importance of some of these qualities varies. For example, accountability is the most important leadership quality in France, Italy, Poland and Russia, while in the UK it was seen as noticeably less important. Although honesty is linked closely to accountability in most countries, it is somewhat less important in Eastern European countries such as Poland, Russia and Hungary. Confidence is seen as a very important quality in the UK, Germany, Italy and Portugal, but less so elsewhere, while focus and inspiration are both ranked particularly highly in Russia.

It seems that managers and leaders are, broadly, meeting the expectations of their employees. Over half of our respondents (56%) believed that their managers exhibited good leadership either most or all of the time, which is good because, as we pointed out earlier, 83% see strong leadership as an important factor in helping them to do their job well. However, 28% only believed they saw the required level of leadership some of the time, and the remaining 16% said they saw it rarely or never. It is important for all HR leaders to ensure that their managers always exhibit good leadership. The results did vary across the continent. Managers in the UK, Russia, Hungary and Portugal were most likely to show good leadership all or most of the time, while those in Italy and Poland were more likely to show it rarely. There is clearly some correlation here with those who see leadership as important to their success, as this was ranked highest in UK, Hungary and Portugal. It might be that their experiences shape how they feel about their performance.

When it comes to the factors that are important when deciding where to work, the countries whose respondents rate their perception of their manager highest are the UK, Russia, Hungary and Portugal – the same ones who believe that their managers show good leadership. This indicates that the positive impression starts early.

We have written earlier in the book that one of the most influential factors for job applicants when deciding which company to join is how a business treats its staff, and the role of managers in the recruitment process seems key to making a positive impression on jobseekers. Once again, applicants in the UK, Hungary and Portugal rate this their highest factor, along with the perception of their manager; perhaps another indicator for their satisfaction with managers showing good leadership. For jobseekers in Russia, it is the company's ambition and growth plans that are most crucial when deciding where to work – which is also a factor that relies on the ability of managers to show strong leadership and belief.

Positive impressions continue into the early period of employment. The top qualities that employees look for in leaders – accountability, honesty, decisiveness and confidence – can be displayed during the interview and the onboarding phases. They are qualities that jobseekers can sense during the interview phase, from the way managers approach their questions and how they talk about their teams and vision for the future. By showing that they are there to support and enable their new hires during onboarding, through building trust, taking a personal interest in the background and aspirations of each new hire, and displaying a more collaborative approach to decision making, they can begin to create the necessary positive impression. The importance of these key qualities in defining great leadership needs to feed into the way a business identifies and develops future managers. Rather than promote purely on a results basis, HR leaders need to design a capability framework that will help identify future managers based on their personal qualities.

The importance of creating a culture of recognition

When employees feel valued by their managers and leaders, they are more likely to be committed and feel engaged. Technology companies such as WorkHuman, O.C. Tanner and Achievers, all of whom have market-leading recognition and engagement software, regularly publish data that supports this. A lack of recognition – whether it be from leaders, managers or colleagues – is one of the three reasons employees give most for leaving an organization. It leads to people feeling undervalued and under-appreciated. The challenge for most leaders is to create a culture in which recognition, and thanks, is hardwired into daily interactions.

In an often-quoted piece of 2016 research from Gallup,[7] employees were asked to remember who had given them their most memorable and meaningful recognition. Just over a quarter (28%) said it came from their manager, and slightly fewer (24%) said it was from a CEO or senior leader. The only other internal source mentioned – by 12% – was their manager's manager (who could have been a senior leader). Of the remaining 36%, around half said it came from a customer or peer, with the remaining half identifying 'other'. It says a lot about the state of recognition culture in our businesses that less than two-thirds of employees receive it from their managers and leaders, and that only one in three of those surveyed had received recognition, or praise, within the previous seven days. Across research sources, less than half of employees say they feel valued by managers and leaders, with almost a third saying they do not feel valued at all by their superiors. A major part of the problem is that recognition, to many leaders, is something they do to engage and retain employees, in other words, a stand-alone initiative aimed at retention when the reality is that recognition, as the major ongoing driver of organizational culture, is something that needs to be integrated into the flow of work itself.

In their 2021 "Global Culture Report"[8] O.C. Tanner found 87% of employees saying that their organization's recognition programme was 'stale, outdated or used as disguised compensation'. This last point is extremely important. Today's modern workforce don't see gratitude or recognition as part of a reward programme but as something they expect to be embedded into organizational culture. In fact, about half of the 87% also believed their recognition programme to be 'disconnected from what is important at the organization'. The report quoted Karen Ackerman, VP of HR for Centra Health, saying 'There is now the expectation that we appreciate great work. Appreciation has become a part of who we are. It's part of the heartbeat of our organization'.

Culture is hugely important to our workforce. Our own research regularly finds that a perceived lack of interest in creating and maintaining a supportive culture from leaders and managers often leads to employee turnover. Research from Glassdoor[9] has also found 'culture and values of the organization' (22%) and 'the quality of senior leadership' (21%) to be the top two factors leading to employee satisfaction. Meanwhile, Achievers' 2020 *Engagement & Retention Report*[10] showed that only 31% of HR leaders believed their organizations have the culture they need for successful growth, with an even smaller proportion – only 21% – believing that their workforce deeply trusted the leaders within the business. While those leaders may have the key role to play in helping to create the right culture for their businesses to succeed, HR leaders themselves also need to take responsibility to see that this is being done. Recognition technology business WorkHuman's co-founder and CEO (Eric Mosley) and Senior VP of Client Strategy & Consulting (Derek Irvine) recently published the book *Making Work Human.*[11] In this they refer to social recognition as 'the practice of people recognising and rewarding each other's efforts, using positive feedback to unlock human potential' which they say lays the foundation for creating a more human workplace. This is because it reinforces shared purpose and gives individuals meaning through gratitude. Moments of gratitude between employees can be powerful and have huge benefits, particularly as it is the employees themselves who effectively are identifying what good performance looks like when they offer gratitude to colleagues in recognition of specific acts. This creates moments that others will try to emulate, while also strengthening human to human interactions. Among the long-term benefits from this form of social recognition are feelings of belonging, connection and engagement. It is democratic (as in, anyone can get involved) and it connects behaviour to organizational culture, purpose and values.

WorkHuman runs an annual survey in collaboration with the Society of Human Resource Managers (SHRM)[12] in the US and finds that HR leaders believe their employee recognition programmes do not just help with organizational culture and organizational values, but also significantly help with employee experience, employee relationships, organizational values, and engagement too. Mosley and Irvine's book concludes that there are three reasons supporting this:

- Recognition makes managing people easier – they say that 'each recognition moment adds to a broader picture of strengths and weaknesses'.

- It strengthens peer-to-peer connection – it is democratic therefore anyone within the business can evaluate performance which reinforces organizational values.

- Business metrics are positively impacted – effective recognition programmes have been proven to drive excellence and reinforce values.

The reality is that recognition isn't an integrated part of organizational culture as yet. O.C. Tanner's report found only 16% of organizations had reached a high level of recognition integration. WorldatWork, a global association of Total Rewards professionals, had similar findings[13] but also uncovered that one in five organizations have no recognition programme at all. To really embed recognition in culture, quite a few things need to happen. We believe the most important ones are:

- Recognizing all efforts, whether large or small, and ensuring that this happens through the whole organization and not individual teams.
- Encouraging frequent peer-to-peer recognition.
- Ensuring that recognition programmes (and the technology that underpins them) are regularly reviewed and improved.
- Connecting employee actions to customer/client outcomes to help them see how they make a difference rather than recognizing them purely for service and internal achievements.

The most impactful recognition is personalized, with O.C. Tanner's research finding 70% of employees saying that it means most to them when that happens.

The concept of modern leadership

At the start of this chapter, we referenced Vineet Nayar and his writings about the difference between leadership and management. Many business writers have explored this in their books. World-renowned author Tom Peters, whose book *In Search of Excellence* has been a business best seller for many years, wrote of how 'Management is about arranging and telling. Leadership is about nurturing and enhancing'. Leadership coach Steve Denning[14] wrote in his book *The Age of Agile* of how previous leadership approaches were a 'steep vertical hierarchy of authority' and that this needs to be replaced with a 'horizontal network of competence, a network composed of self-organizing teams'. He also writes that previous approaches to leadership cannot address complexity, nor the rapid pace of change we have seen in the digital age. This change has seen a focus on customer needs, sometimes at the expense of employee needs. Previous approaches to leadership may have involved telling people what to do and trying to coerce change, however, as we have seen, digital

talent wants something different. They are motivated by opportunities for growth, development and achievement, so leaders need to
inspire a culture of support and enablement – and as we have just
seen in the last section – recognition and appreciation. The other
thing that leaders need to create is a sense of connection. Modern
leaders are expected to engage both the brain and the heart of their
workers. O.C. Tanner's 2021 Global Culture Report focuses heavily
on leadership. Their research shows modern leaders to be 'effective,
progressive and emotionally intelligent', rejecting command and
control in favour of focusing on 'coaching, developing and empowering their people to do great work'. The traits they exhibit include
collaborative approaches, connecting their people to a greater sense
of purpose, an openness about information sharing, a belief in inclusion and a thriving culture.

Of course, a lot of this is aspirational for most businesses. *Fortune*
magazine's CEO survey[15] in 2017/18 found only 7% of CEOs thinking they are developing effective leaders, while a similar survey found
only 21% of employees believing their managers effectively led them.
Research from Deloitte and The Female Quotient[16] in 2019 asked
employees what they saw as the most important qualities of a leader.
The nine that people identified (in descending order of importance)
were:

- giving credit where its due;
- listening attentively;
- accountability;
- purposeful;
- good communicators;
- strong work ethic;
- flexible;
- confident;
- patient.

Our own research (quoted in an earlier section in this chapter) uncovered similar results. However, what was interesting in this research

was the role that inclusivity and authenticity played. We know that employees increasingly do not respond to autocratic leaders but instead want a range of perspectives and experiences to be heard and integrated. They want leaders who will 'have their back' if something goes wrong, and who can create and foster strong values and a real sense of camaraderie among workers, and importantly also be transparent and aware of their own personal weaknesses. In fact, around two-thirds look for leaders to create camaraderie within the business, being as open with information and recognition as possible.

The O.C. Tanner report uses the metaphor of a business leader as a conductor of an orchestra, quoting classical music journalist Tom Service,[17] who has written a book on the importance of the conductor. He points out that the work of a conductor is not about establishing authority but creating 'a culture of responsibility, of respect, of musical and social awareness, and of listening'. He uses connection as a metaphor for shared experiences and collaboration. We also think this metaphor is very useful when trying to understand the differences between modern, digital leadership and older, more autocratic approaches.

In 2020, the global management training business Hemsley Fraser published a set of leadership traits that they believe are needed for the modern digital workforce, under the heading of *Leadership in the Balance*. While the title may seem a bit apocalyptic, we're sure that a different approach to leadership will thrive in the digital age. The traits they identified show both the complexity that modern leaders face, but also how and why leadership in the digital age can be an evolving and adaptable practice rather than rigid and autocratic. For example, curiosity, critical thinking, vulnerability and confidence may not automatically seem like traditional leadership traits. However, for businesses moving forward, the need to analyze, reflect, investigate and embrace uncertainty are all vital for leaders who wish to gain the confidence and respect of their people. It is important for them to be empathetic towards employees and their concerns, but not at the expense of being decisive when difficult calls must be made. Leaders need to be brave enough to challenge and disrupt their businesses when necessary, but in a way that still engages their people. Change can be unsettling for employees, so it needs to be approached carefully to get their buy-in. The report identifies technology as offering the best ways to keep employees engaged and informed during change, specifically referencing digitally facilitated focus groups, pulse surveys, on-demand learning and better communication tools. Creativity among the workforce needs to be encouraged, but results must come with it. Leaders cannot be seen to stifle their people but will need to project manage them in a way that will deliver results.

Perhaps two of the most important traits for modern leaders are agility and attention. The need to constantly adapt and adjust business approaches, while also continually remaining on top of technological advances and changing client and consumer expectations, will need to be balanced by an attention to detail that stabilizes the business strategy and prevents any distractions or the chance of succumbing to 'shiny new tools' thinking.

The leadership challenges of digital transformation

As we are writing in this book about the impact of digital transformation on businesses it is important to stress that leaders of businesses who are facing digital disruption within their own sectors need to be bold. In October 2018 McKinsey published a report on the digital strategy which they said, by its nature, could never be incremental. They broke down the areas in which they believed leaders may face resistance from within their own businesses, requiring them to be bold in their approach to influencing and inspiring their people. The first challenge is what they called ignorance. By that, they mean a lack of understanding within the business about how they can become more profitable and successful through digitization. This will often lead to a 'shiny new object' approach in which managers and leaders adopt the latest tools or platforms, without considering their impact or employee needs, and potentially resulting in missed commercial opportunities and employee dissatisfaction.

Back in Chapter 1, we wrote of how organizations need to 'create a whole new business infrastructure designed to innovate, restructure and consistently lead the way in consumer expectations'. Leaders need to see this vision and be able to influence and inspire their managers and employees to share it. This will involve improving their own knowledge of digital platforms and how they can be used, and look where digital technologies might be changing the economic landscape for their sector or service.

The second challenge for leaders is to combat inertia. Most managers and decision-makers may fear the impact of a digital change on their own parts of the business and their ability to influence their teams, which might result in them looking to maintain the status quo. Leaders need to have an honest dialogue and to address fears and insecurities, potentially creating support networks and involving external experts to explain the changing landscape. The third challenge is around what the authors of the McKinsey report called guesswork. Digitization represents a leap into the unknown for most businesses, bringing with it ambiguity and uncertainty, which can create a tendency to embrace guesswork. The role of leaders is to oversee a transition that limits the guesswork and slowly builds proof points using data-driven insights. The fourth challenge is the diffusion of effort that usually comes when trying to do two things at once – in this case, it refers to businesses that are trying to reinvent their own internal processes through digitization while at the same time attempting to digitize their external offerings to remain competitive. Leaders need to combat a lack of overall focus by reallocating resources and studying what their competitors are doing, something made easier by a proliferation of information and data about what has and hasn't worked for a variety of businesses.

We believe that these types of challenges can only be met by leaders who are inspirational and influential, and open to new ways of thinking and different ideas. Leadership in the digital age – whether it is about leading a whole organization or a small team – is complex and fast-moving, but the rewards for those who can really embrace it are huge.

Leadership in the spotlight – the need
for transparent governance

In the opening section of this chapter, we reported on how the general public was looking towards private business for guidance, and how research indicated that people looked towards leaders to help fix problems, putting business leadership firmly in the spotlight. It is true that leadership in the digital age is under more scrutiny than ever before. There is far more awareness of governance at both a corporate and political level. Digital communication platforms make it easier for employees to call out bad management practices and for companies to become instantly aware of the potential ramifications of their commercial decisions to a more sceptical and informed public. Senior managers and directors are also using these platforms to communicate, sometimes with less than successful results. For example, in the UK, during the summer of 2021, a former government adviser published some of his confidential WhatsApp message threads with the prime minister, mostly concerning government decisions.[18] It is not hard to imagine an ex-senior manager from a business doing something similar. Conversations, decisions and future plans that are discussed using private channels can now easily be made public, opening management up to scrutiny and accountability that it has previously not had to consider.

Just as consumers have learned that they can quickly take to social media platforms to call out poor service or shoddy workmanship, so our employees can also voice their concerns over working conditions. As we have said earlier in the book – your employer brand is what your employees experience, and therefore what they say it is, rather than what an organization says about itself. There are many examples of employees – be they ex or current – calling out the practices of their businesses through social platforms. This can occur on LinkedIn, through poor reviews on Glassdoor, or in private (and sometimes not so private) Facebook groups. Sometimes these can lead to action being taken. In June 2021, a letter written by ex-employees of the British craft brewing firm Brewdog went viral through social media and was featured on news bulletins and in newspapers.[19]

In the letter, 61 ex-employees complained of how the company's rapid growth had been achieved by 'cutting corners on health and safety' and creating a 'toxic culture that left staff suffering from mental illness'. The company has been a commercial success in the brewing sector, becoming the UK's fastest-growing drinks company in 2016. In response to the viral letter, the business was forced into a contrite response. It wasn't the first time that the business had received negative PR around its culture. In 2016 they were featured in a BBC programme called *Who's the Boss*. The aim of the series was to hand the recruitment of a key member of staff over to the workforce themselves, without senior management becoming involved, to see the type of person and background that the workers would choose. After all, they know the job best and the ground truth around any problems that the new hire may need to address. The fact that such a series was made and aired on a major terrestrial channel in a prime-time slot further indicates how transparent business and leadership has become. Such a programme also offers the public a counterbalance to more autocratic business programmes like *The Apprentice*, and offers more of an insight into how businesses are run. In the episode featuring Brewdog however, one of the co-founders took over the recruiting process and made the final decision as he didn't believe his workforce would choose the 'right' person. He made the offer to his preferred candidate, and then had his offer rejected. As the programme finished, the co-founder tweeted 'Well, that was a bit of a disaster'.[20] The emerging workforce is savvy and principled. As we said in the last section, they have ecological, political and sociological concerns and want to work for organizations that recognize this. They have views on fairness – be it the fairness of opportunity or fairness in decision making. This makes modern leaders more accountable to their people, with this accountability creating expectations of action when something is not perceived to be right or fair. We've often been told that the younger workforce wants to work for businesses whose purpose they align with, but this goes much deeper than merely market positioning. It goes to the heart of how decisions are made, how accountable the decision-makers are, and to whom. They want to see accountability for their leaders and managers. This accountability is for all leaders in all organizations, great and small. In August 2021 a website was launched called *Apple Too*.[21] The aim was to use it to collect stories from current and former workers at Apple, at all levels, who have 'experienced harassment or discrimination'. It is too early for us to know how this will develop, and what action may eventually be taken, but suffice to say, in the digital age it seems that poor leadership practice will get called out. As we begin to address the environmental and sociological challenges our businesses face (and in the UK establish the post-Brexit legal and economic landscape) there will be a renewed focus on who our partners, suppliers and collaborators are. How have they been appointed or engaged? In whose interests are they operating? How were they selected, and do they have any connections to anyone involved in the decision-making process?

Our employees tend to know the ground truths of how their company is performing. They have 'skin in the game' when it comes to either successful growth or poor commercial performance and they know they will be impacted by the consequences of either. They can see with their own eyes how diverse their companies are when recruiting, how supportive they are when colleagues need help, and whether individuals are getting the opportunities for growth and development that they expected.

Transparent governance requires modern leaders to operate in a way that offers greater clarity, stability and accountability to their people and shows that they can deliver on promises of being a great place to work. With leadership in the spotlight, their responses to external events will often become public and open to analysis by everyone from employees and customers to the business and general media.

Those working within organizations expect the mix of colleagues to be representative of the world they live in. We have already referenced the business response to the increased prominence of the Black Lives Matter movement, and in the next chapter, we shall explore in more depth how businesses are approaching, and embracing, the need for greater diversity, equity, inclusion and belonging.

Chapter summary

In this chapter, we have seen that leaders increasingly need to be seen as being influential, inspirational and motivational for their workforce, many of whom see strong leadership as an important factor in helping them to do their job well. Key points to consider here are:

- Modern leaders are not expected to be autocratic decision-makers, but to be confident, honest and accountable.

- Employees want to feel valued by their leaders and expect to receive recognition from them.

- Employee turnover tends to increase when there is a perceived lack of interest from leaders in creating and maintaining a supportive culture.

- Modern leaders are expected to engage both the brain and the heart of their people through coaching, developing and empowering them.

- Leading a business through a digital transformation can be challenging as it brings ambiguity and uncertainty to the workforce. Leaders need to win hearts and minds with data and influence.

- Transparent governance is important to our digital workforce. Modern digital communication channels can and will be used to call out questionable leadership practices.

Endnotes

1 V Nayar, Three Differences Between Managers and Leaders, *Harvard Business Review*, 2 August 2013, hbr.org/2013/08/tests-of-a-leadership-transiti (archived at https://perma.cc/XXS4-PH97)

2 Edelman. Trust Barometer, www.edelman.com/trust/2021-trust-barometer (archived at https://perma.cc/3HWA-F9YC)

3 O.C.Tanner Institute. *Global Culture Report*, www.octanner.com/content/dam/oc-tanner/images/v2/culture-report/2021/GCR-2021-sm.pdf (archived at https://perma.cc/87CA-9FDK).1

4 PWC. PWC 24th Annual Global CEO Survey, www.pwc.com/gx/en/ceo-agenda/ceosurvey/2021.html (archived at https://perma.cc/J2JA-KKQN)

5   Deloitte. 2021 Fortune/Deloitte CEO Survey, www2.deloitte.com/us/en/pages/
chief-executive-officer/articles/ceo-survey.html (archived at https://perma.cc/
8K6T-FNP3)

6   L Poonamallee. We have a massive opportunity to determine the future of
leadership right now, Fast Company, 29 June 2021. www.fastcompany.com/
90650709/we-have-a-massive-opportunity-determine-the-future-of-leadership-
right-now (archived at https://perma.cc/6MU6-UPGA)

7   A Mann and N Dvorak. Employee Recognition: Low Cost, High Impact, *Gallup*,
28 June 2016. www.gallup.com/workplace/236441/employee-recognition-low-
cost-high-impact.aspx (archived at https://perma.cc/BVU2-VPBH)

8   O.C.Tanner. Recognition, www.octanner.com/global-culture-report/2021/
recognition.html?utm_source=twitter&utm_medium=social&utm_
campaign=us.2021.jul.article.gcr (archived at https://perma.cc/5K5K-R2PC)

9   P Wong. Does More Money Change What We Value at Work? Glass Door,
17 January 2017. www.glassdoor.com/research/more-money-change-value-at-
work (archived at https://perma.cc/556S-WU4L)

10 Achievers. Empowerment & Trust: Create a Culture of Feedback with
Employee Listening, 18 December 2020. resources.achievers.com/resources/
empowerment-and-trust-the-keys-to-employee-engagement/ (archived at
https://perma.cc/85QN-FPSW)

11 E Mosley and D Irvine (2020) *Making Work Human: How Human-Centered
Companies are Changing the Future of Work and the World*, McGraw-Hill
Education, London

12 WorkHuman. 2018 SHRM/WorkHuman Employee Recognition Survey, www.
workhuman.com/resources/papers/findings-from-the-2018-shrm-workhuman-
employee-recognition-survey-designing-work-cultures-for-the-human-era
(archived at https://perma.cc/7HNX-DCVG)

13 V Bolden-Barrett. Study: Organizations are torn on employee recognition
programs, HR Dive, 24 June 2019. www.hrdive.com/news/study-
organizations-are-torn-on-employee-recognition-programs/557382/ (archived
at https://perma.cc/QN56-56SG)

14 S Denning. Why Mindset Is Driving The Age Of Agile, *Forbes*, 20 August
2018. www.forbes.com/sites/stevedenning/2018/08/20/why-mindset-
is-driving-the-age-of-agile/?sh=32d94ca95631 (archived at https://perma.cc/
GG8U-CPEE)

15 Deloitte. 2021 Fortune/Deloitte CEO Survey, www2.deloitte.com/us/en/pages/
chief-executive-officer/articles/ceo-survey.html (archived at https://perma.cc/
YF3W-BRPG)

16 Deloitte. Deloitte and The Female Quotient Alliance, www2.deloitte.com/us/
en/pages/about-deloitte/articles/the-female-quotient.html (archived at https://
perma.cc/7GDS-KPV9)

17 BBC Radio 3. What's the Point of the Conductor?, *The Listening Service*, 4 November 2018. www.bbc.co.uk/programmes/b08qtdts (archived at https://perma.cc/795D-YWN8)

18 E Webber. The perils of Boris Johnson's government by WhatsApp, *Politico*, 18 June 2021. www.politico.eu/article/dominic-cummings-screenshots-reveal-boris-johnson-government-by-whatsapp/ (archived at https://perma.cc/24U3-LRLX)

19 K Makortoff and R Davies. Former BrewDog staff accuse craft beer firm of culture of fear, *The Guardian*, 10 June 2021. www.theguardian.com/business/2021/jun/10/brewdog-staff-craft-beer-firm-letter (archived at https://perma.cc/C79T-BDQB)

20 J McCarthy. BrewDog boss James Watt dubs BBC Who's the Boss appearance 'a bit of a disaster', *The Drum*, 9 March 2016. www.thedrum.com/news/2016/03/09/brewdog-boss-james-watt-dubs-bbc-who-s-boss-appearance-bit-disaster (archived at https://perma.cc/7TGP-UJT4)

21 Z Schiffer. Apple employees are organizing, now under the banner #AppleToo, *The Verge*, 23 August 2021. www.theverge.com/2021/8/23/22638150/apple-appletoo-employee-harassment-discord (archived at https://perma.cc/F752-4CR6)

06

Diversity and inclusion

In previous chapters, we have seen that the talent challenges facing companies in this time of accelerated digital transformation are complex, multifaceted and, in some cases, seemingly insurmountable. In this chapter, we will look at diversity and inclusion issues and how the renewed efforts being made to solve them can also go a long way to solving the broader digital talent challenges that employers are facing.

Before the events of 2020, it was already clear that building a more diverse workforce was a growing priority for many employers around the world. Diversity and inclusion have never had a more prominent place as topics in conference programmes. It is clear that HR and talent acquisition professionals are taking them very seriously. This is not surprising as embracing diversity, and most critically inclusion, opens up new talent pools, drives diversity of thought within organizations and helps companies better reflect their communities and the customers they serve.

The death of George Floyd in May 2020, the subsequent global protests, and the rise of the Black Lives Matter movement have heralded greater scrutiny on diversity, equity and inclusion in all aspects of society. As a result, many employers have now made commitments to be anti-racist, and the focus on diversity and inclusion in the workforce is ever more intense. However, what has become clear is that, despite many years of seemingly purposeful effort, many employers' existing diversity and inclusion initiatives have failed to make a meaningful difference.

Research that we worked on in partnership with Avado in the latter part of 2019[1] illustrated that, despite significant lip service, diversity was less of a focus for senior leadership than it was perceived to be. When asked how important they felt it was to have a diverse workforce, only 31% of senior leaders saw diversity as highly important and 29% as very important. This left 40% of senior leadership who either saw diversity as one of several talent challenges or, in a small number of cases, something they weren't interested in at all. Unsurprisingly then, when we asked talent acquisition leaders how happy they were with the way their organization approaches diversity, just over half (53%) said they were happy but felt that their business could do more. A third said they were happy and felt their companies were doing well, and 14% were unhappy, saying that it needed greater priority. Looking at it another way, two-thirds (67%) feel that to varying degrees, their organizations could do better in their approach to diversity.

More recent research from the Josh Bersin Academy,[2] undertaken in November 2020, illustrates an unsurprising but nevertheless fairly limited shift in leadership attitudes. The research reported that 65% of senior leaders said they felt diversity was good for business. Worryingly though, the research showed that the gap between what leaders say and what leaders do persists, with only 39% having diversity, equity and inclusion as an integral part of their business strategy and only 25% setting any kind of DE&I targets and quotas. The Bersin research also sheds some light on something that is at the crux of the issue; only 12% of the senior leaders they asked were rewarded or recognized for reaching DE&I goals. It is evident that many organizations still have much work to do, and the real-world consequences of their corporate inaction are significant. For example, research from recruiting technology company Headstart undertaken in October of 2020 revealed that in a survey of 400 hiring managers in the USA, 38% of hiring managers admitted to discriminating against a job seeker because of their race, age, gender, disability, sexual orientation, religion or for another reason.

In her book, *Authentic Diversity*[3] Michelle Silverthorn, diversity expert and CEO of Inclusion Nation, talks about the changing rules of diversity and why a reliance on some unwritten 'old rules' has led to the failure of diversity programmes. She identifies these old rules as reoccurring tropes such as: 'Make the business case for diversity and inclusion. Money talks. Don't make anyone too uncomfortable. Don't be too radical with your ideas for change. Don't be too honest. Don't tell anyone they're wrong'. For successful inclusion and belonging to occur, these old rules need to be replaced. So how do organizations need to think differently about diversity and inclusion, how do the elements of the problem break down, and how can genuinely improving diversity and inclusion also help solve digital talent challenges? We will look at the issues and some of the successful solutions in detail in this chapter, and where better to start than by taking a deeper dive into the advantages of diverse organizations.

The advantages of diverse organizations

The commercial advantages of diversity within organizations have been known and documented for a long time. Research from McKinsey[4] in 2015 found that companies with more diverse top teams are also top financial performers, being 21% more profitable than those who are not diverse. They also make better, faster decisions.

More recent McKinsey research[5] reveals that those companies whose executive teams were in the top quartile for gender diversity were 27% more likely to outperform the others on profitability. Likewise, companies with executive teams in the top quartile for ethnic/cultural diversity were 33% more likely to have 'industry-leading profitability'. In McKinsey's words: 'That this relationship continues to be strong suggests that inclusion of highly diverse individuals – and the myriad ways in which diversity exists beyond gender (e.g. LGBTQ+, age/generation, international experience) – can be a key differentiator among companies'. McKinsey also highlights the dangers of 'opting out'. Companies in the bottom quartile for gender and ethnic/cultural diversity were 29% less likely to achieve profitability that was above average: 'In short, not only were they not leading, they were lagging'. Profitability isn't the only advantage to be gained by more diverse organizations. Research from Boston Consulting Group and the Technical University of Munich[6] illustrates that companies with the greatest gender diversity generated around 34% of their overall revenue from innovative products and services. The report concludes that:

> The evidence also suggests that having a high percentage of female managers is positively correlated with disruptive innovation, in which a new product, service, or business model fully replaces the version that existed before (such as what Netflix has done to DVD rental stores and what Amazon is doing to retail).

This type of disruptive innovation is critical to companies that want to succeed in digital transformation.

The other key advantage of a robust diversity hiring strategy is the opening up of additional valuable pools of talent to bring critical skills into the organization. Accenture's disability inclusion research report[7] indicates that 15.1 million people of working age live with disabilities in the US and suggest that by embracing disability inclusion, companies would unlock access to a talent pool containing more than 10.7 million people. Increasing the size of the pool of available talent unsurprisingly brings considerable financial benefits. Accenture reports that 'Companies that have improved their inclusion of persons with disabilities over time were four times more likely than others to have total shareholder returns that outperform those of their peer group'. One important factor that sits behind the commercial and disruptive power of diverse organizations is the way that including people from diverse backgrounds can help to drive cognitive diversity. In his book *Rebel Ideas* journalist Matthew Syed talks about the importance of thinking about human performance from the standpoint of the group rather than the individual and identifies cognitive diversity as a 'critical ingredient of driving "collective intelligence"'. Identifying that there is often an overlap between demographic diversity and cognitive diversity, he suggests that 'people from different backgrounds, with different experience, often think about problems in different ways'. As well as potentially affecting a company's reputation and long-term performance, a lack of diversity can create bias in data and algorithms. Findings from an NYU research centre published last year[8] showed that a lack of diversity within artificial intelligence, in particular, can create flawed systems perpetuating gender and racial biases. There are well-documented examples of chatbots mimicking hate speech and image recognition software classifying minorities offensively. Early in 2020, it was reported[9] that Amazon's facial recognition technology, which is marketed to police departments, has difficulty identifying the gender of female and darker-skinned faces. There are also social media mentions of a health chatbot that only recognizes heart attack symptoms in men – any women describing their symptoms might not have the urgency of their situation recognized.

Furthermore, a lack of diversity in product design can have grave physical consequences. An often-cited example is from automotive design and safety. Traditionally, automotive products were primarily designed by men, and when the first crash test dummies were developed in the 1960s, they were similarly modelled on average male height, weight and stature. As a consequence of this bias in design and testing, cars were manufactured that were largely unsafe for women. In fact, female drivers were 47% more likely to be seriously injured in a car crash. Eventually, in 2011, female crash test dummies were required.

The examples above represent just a tiny snapshot from the considerable body of compelling evidence linking business performance to diversity and inclusion. So why then haven't companies seen improving diversity as an obvious way of improving their organization and prioritized it as a solution to drive transformation?

As illustrated by the research cited earlier, the current lack of board-level accountability is undoubtedly a critical factor here, but if companies are to take full advantage of successfully building diverse workforces it is also vital to understand the deep-rooted nature and complexity of the issues.

A systemic problem

One of the key issues that the events of 2020 have shone a new light on is the prevalence of bias baked into our work and life systems. One of the most critical reasons diversity hiring initiatives are unsuccessful is their failure to take into account and address this deep systemic bias. To understand the nature of this bias further and its impact on digital talent, let's take the example of the underrepresentation of women working in the technology sector. The technology sector lags significantly behind other industries in terms of gender diversity, with two-thirds of boards and 40% of senior leadership teams having no female representation. In 2018, women only accounted for 16% of the total IT workforce, even though they represent half of the customer base. According to Accenture, women hold just 16% of engineering roles and 27% of computing roles in companies in the US. It would be easy to look at these numbers and point to bias in the recruitment process, and although, as we'll see later, this is undoubtedly a key issue, the systemic bias that significantly contributes to this problem actually starts in the education system. In 2020 figures from the Joint Council of Qualifications[10] reported a 21.8% increase in girls studying computing at A-Level. On the surface, this would seem to be significant progress and a sign of the success of recent campaigns to get more girls taking STEM subjects at school. However, this one statistic doesn't tell the whole story as girls represented only 14% of the number of students taking the qualification. Although progress is being made, computing is still very much a male-dominated subject in British schools. It logically follows that the same is true at the university level, with only 16.2% of computer science degree students being female in 2020. This was only a 1% increase on the previous year indicating that these problems are still a long way from being solved. So why is this the case? In the past, the biological differences in cognitive ability have been suggested, with girls having an intrinsic aptitude for verbal recall and writing and boys having an intrinsic aptitude for spatial and numerical tasks, but in recent decades research has thoroughly debunked this. For example, Professor Elizabeth Spelke from Harvard University indicated in an article for *American Psychologist* back in 2006[11] that research on infants, children and students of all ages 'provides evidence that mathematical and scientific reasoning develops from a set of biologically based cognitive capacities that males and females share. These capacities lead men and women to develop equal talent for mathematics and science'. The research points to the main cause of the problem being socially constructed gender stereotypes that kick in at a very young age. Recent research from a group of American psychologists revealed that gender stereotypes about ability and 'brilliance' can be cemented in children by the age of six. The Organisation for Economic Co-operation and Development's Programme for International Student Assessment found[12] that girls tend to underachieve against boys when asked to 'think like scientists'. Tellingly they have also identified that parents are more likely to expect their sons rather than their daughters to have a career in technology, engineering or maths' fields. Such subject-specific stereotyping leads to fewer girls taking STEM subjects, which in turn affects the pool of qualified digital talent available to employers. This creates a vicious circle where a lack of female role models in technology careers helps to reinforce these stereotypes for the next generation. This stereotyping is both caused by and acts to reinforce systemic bias. Overcoming bias both on an institutional and individual level is vital if employers are to build a diverse and inclusive business. However, doing so effectively is a considerable challenge. Conscious or explicit bias should be easy to spot and deal with. Indeed, government legislation makes many types of bias and discrimination illegal in the workplace. Unfortunately, although overt discrimination still exists, laws on discrimination are not consistent across borders, and those laws do not always protect all minority groups. By its very nature, unconscious bias is hard to spot, and dealing with it can be very challenging. The University of California give this explanation of unconscious bias:[13]

> Unconscious biases are social stereotypes about certain groups of people that individuals form outside their own conscious awareness. Everyone holds unconscious beliefs about various social and identity groups, and these biases stem from one's tendency to organize social worlds by categorizing.

Unconscious bias is far more prevalent than conscious prejudice and often incompatible with one's conscious values.

Unconscious bias is a massive problem in recruiting and a significant barrier standing in the way of the considerable benefits a more diverse workforce would bring both to employers and to society as a whole. Moreover, these implicit biases don't just operate on an individual basis; they also get codified by corporate cultures.

In Chapter 3, we spoke about the need for diverse thinking to drive digital transformation and the negative implications of credentialism, outdated recruiting practices and the prevalence of recruiting for culture fit when it comes to hiring diverse teams. Many experts are now pointing at the concept of culture fit as being one of the most culpable factors that codify unconscious bias within organizations.

In a recent interview on the *Recruiting Future* podcast, Bret Putter, the CEO of Culture Gene and the author of a number of books on company culture, has this to say about hiring for culture fit:[14]

> There's no such thing as culture fit. When I ask a leader to accurately describe their culture, they can't. Maybe they may waffle about their mission and their values, but that's not your culture. Your culture is this random combination of good and bad behaviours, norms, principles, habits, beliefs, communication styles, operating styles, different departments, subcultures etc etc… It's impossible to define. So, if you can't define it, how can you recruit for it? What's happened is that people have come up with this cool-sounding phrase for what is really just gut instinct or intuition. If it's your gut instinct, then your biases will be deciding whether it feels like this person will work well in the organization.

Kevin Wheeler, the founder of The Future Of Talent Institute, an experienced researcher and commentator on talent acquisition, has this to say on culture fit and unconscious bias:[15]

> It is impossible to have a single comprehensive definition of culture and use it to screen candidates objectively. Culture and cultural fit are too complex to be defined well or unearthed in an interview or through a test.

I am concerned that recruiters and hiring managers use a simplistic definition of corporate culture and cultural fit to reinforce their own biases. Hiring managers, recruiters and senior leaders have stereotypes about what makes a good candidate. They have beliefs about cultural background, education levels, schools people attended, grades achieved and activities participated in. They may favour people from one organization over another. One set of corporate values may say that energy and passion are critical. And then, we decide that the male candidate is energetic and a go-getter but that the woman is overly aggressive. Or that young candidates have more energy and willingness to go the extra mile than do older ones.

Unconscious bias is damaging enough in individuals who are recruiting for organizations, but both Brett and Kevin are clear that it is often codified into the entire organization. This creates a vicious circle because as companies grow, they unconsciously or often even consciously recruit more people who fit their definition of culture fit, solidifying bias, stifling diversity and making it more challenging to solve the problem. However, unfortunately, this doesn't just apply to individual organizations; entire industries continue reinforcing biased hiring methodologies under the auspices of stereotypes and culture. An exploration of deeply encoded gender bias in technology offers a clear illustration of how this works. We have already seen that the technology sector has a huge problem with gender diversity. This has led to a big focus on gender equality in hiring by some employers, examples of which we will see later in the chapter. However, despite the light being shone on the problem and a focus on many places to fix it, gender representation in the technology sector has actually gone backwards. As Accenture point out:

> It's a startling truth: In spite of the efforts many have made in the last decade toward encouraging girls and women to pursue technology careers, the percentage of tech workers who were women in 1984 (35%) was actually higher than it is today (32%).

This reduction in female representation is something that chimes with my father Ray Alder's experiences from his career, which surfed the wave of the growth of business computing over four decades. Ray started his IT career as an apprentice in the data processing department at Hotpoint in the early 1960s, working on tabulators that read digital data stored on stiff pieces of paper known as punch cards. He recalls that 100% of the staff working in the punch card room to produce the cards were female, and the majority of tabulators were also run by women who had previously either been accounts' clerks or part of the typing pool. As the industry moved towards electronic tabulators, which worked from electrical pulses, the job of the programmer was created, and while my Dad recalls that many of the best programmers were women, this shift in technology saw more men entering the data processing industry. This trend continued as 'data processing' morphed into 'information technology' and eventually became the digital technology industry that we know today. My father's observations are also evidence of much that has been researched and documented about the role of women in technology, illustrating similar trends in the US to those my Dad was witnessing in the UK during the 60s, 70s and 80s.

Many of the pioneers of computer programming have been women. Ada Lovelace is credited as being the first computer programmer back in the 1840s, being the first person to publish an algorithm designed to be read by the Analytical Engine, the first modern computer. This trend continued through influential women like Grace Hopper, a pioneer of computer programming in the 1950s and Margaret Hamilton, director of the team at MIT who created the Apollo moon landing software in 1969. In 1967, *Cosmopolitan* ran an article titled 'The Rise Of The Computer Girls', illustrating what a lucrative career computer programming could be for women.

So, what changed? In the early 1960s, computing was expanding way beyond the existing experienced programmer talent pool, and companies were having to find ways of assessing the potential of trainees. The most popular tool to do this was the IBM Programmer Aptitude Test. The test focused on problem-solving skills and was the industry standard for many years. As the industry grew, the search for potential talent intensified, and companies looked at new ways of expanding the talent pool. In her book *Brotopia: Breaking Up The Boys Club Of Silicon Valley,* tech journalist Emily Chang writes about the Programmer Scale personality test designed by William Cannon and Dallis Perry, two male psychologists working for the company System Development Corporation. The test was built by profiling the interests of 1,378 programmers to build a scale that would predict the level of satisfaction people would have with programming as a career. Unfortunately, only 186 of the programmers profiled were women. While some of the findings were reasonably logical (people who like solving mathematical problems made good programmers), one of their main conclusions was that programmers satisfied with their career choice share the characteristic of not liking people. As Emily Chang says:

> If you select for an antisocial nerd stereotype, you will hire more men and fewer women; that's what the research tells us. The prevalence of antisocial personality disorder, for instance, favours men by a three-to-one ratio.

These types of tests were used well into the 1980s and have birthed a stereotype about programmers that still persists nearly 60 years after they were first devised.

Baking bias into assessment is unfortunately not just a historical problem; in fact, the recent rise of technology powered by algorithms and artificial intelligence has created the potential for bias to be magnified on an massive scale. Automated bias is becoming a big issue, with some of the tech industries' biggest names being called out for using AI technology that acts in a racist or sexist way. In September of 2020, Twitter was forced to apologize[16] when hundreds of Twitter users highlighted that its image cropping algorithm was behaving in a racist way and automatically focusing on the white faces in images. This wasn't the first time something like this has happened. Back in 2015, Google was forced to apologize when its Photos software automatically tagged two black faces as gorillas. Twitter claimed to have tested its algorithm before it went live and found no evidence of gender or racial bias but, based on the findings of its users, conceded it had more testing to do. Considering how easy it was to replicate the issue, many argue that this seriously calls Twitter's testing methodology into question and perhaps highlights a deeper systematic problem in the world of artificial intelligence.

Earlier in the chapter, we talked about the dangers of a lack of diversity in product design, and this is absolutely a case in point. In early 2021, the Alan Turing Institute in the UK released a report entitled 'Where are the women? Mapping the gender job gap in AI'. Their research identified that there is a 'troubling and persistent absence of women employed in the Artificial Intelligence (AI) and Data Science fields'. They report that fewer than a quarter of professionals in these areas globally are women, and in the UK, the percentage of women drops to 20%. This leads to significant problems with 'a feedback loop shaping gender bias in AI and machine learning systems'.

There is a significant danger that as these technologies become more widespread in the recruiting process, the issue becomes a self-replicating vicious circle. There is already some early evidence of this happening. For example, in 2018, a large technology company was widely reported to have abandoned the development of an AI recruiting tool that automatically screened CVs to help them quickly identify the best talent. The tool was found to be actively screening out women for software development and technical roles because it was basing its selection on the applications of previous successful candidates to those jobs. These successful applications were disproportionately male because, as we have seen, these types of roles are disproportionately filled by males. The examples we have used to illustrate systemic bias and its effect of limiting the pool of digital talent have been based on gender, but it is critically important to have an intersectional understanding of the workplace. Ethnicity, parental status, socio-economic status, neurodiversity, sexuality and disability are areas where conscious, unconscious and systemic bias is causing discrimination that holds back diversity in many workplaces.

Inclusion

Before we start to look at the ways employers are solving some of the issues we have discussed, it is imperative that we recognize that diversity in hiring is only a fraction of the overall issue. While diversity and inclusion are always paired together in conversations about talent, it is fair to say, certainly historically, that diversity has always tended to get the most focus. This lack of focus on inclusion is a key contributing issue to the lack of diversity in many organizations. In their recent research into building inclusive workforces, the CIPD has this to say on inclusion: 'Hiring a diverse workforce doesn't guarantee that every employee has the same experience or opportunities in the workplace. Inclusion is what's needed to give diversity real impact, and drive towards a world of work where all employees are empowered to thrive'.[17] They go on to talk about the importance of seeing inclusion as being fundamentally based on a focus on individual experience, which allows everyone to be productive and feel that they belong within the organization. This sense of the importance of individuality is something that is echoed by diversity and inclusion consultant Jackie Glenn who was formerly global chief diversity officer at EMC. Speaking on the *Recruiting Future* podcast,[18] she highlights how inclusivity is an issue for many organizations: 'It's not just about how you recruit people. Once I get there, what are you going to do to retain me? How are you going to make me feel like I belong there? Are you going to make sure you treat me equitably and I think many companies haven't grasped that yet. When you think of diversity, it's individually; it's who you are.' She also echoes the CIPD on inclusion: 'inclusion is making sure that everyone gets their voice heard. Everyone is included you just don't recruit me just to add diversity at [to] your company and then leave me in a corner and don't ask me for my opinion, don't involve me in anything and really just want me there because I make the landscape looked different.'

However, it's not just inclusion that is important here; equity and belonging are also critical. Jackie says:

> Inclusion is making sure I feel included, and equity is also making sure I'm being treated equitably. A lot of feedback that we get from women

and underrepresented minorities is that they are not invited to give their input and [if] they do it is sometimes frowned upon when they speak. Belonging is making someone feel that the company is their company, they have a stake and the leadership make them feel like they belong there.

The issue for many organizations is that equity, inclusion and belonging have to be part of a culture in the business that comes from the top of the organization. It is not something a special project or initiative can create or fix; it goes much deeper than that. Global communication and branding leader Charu Malhotra describes the role of leadership like this:

> Traditional leaders, up until very recently were trained to look at people as resources to get the work done. Whereas if you think about employee experience and keeping people engaged, that's a very different leadership model. That means that we have to look at work as a resource to build people to retain people, to engage people.

Recognition is critical here, but recognition is also something that is very individual. As Charu says: 'Whatever you're doing, whether you're working on the shop floor, whether you're working in a call centre, whether you're in the C-suite, you want to feel valued, you want to be motivated, you want to be engaged, you want recognition but how we want recognition differs from person to person'. Ultimately effective inclusion, equity and belonging come down to creating a culture where people can bring their whole selves to work, are respected for who they are and the contribution they can make. Charu has some important thoughts on this:

> if we have to bring a mask into work, if we have to operate in a way that hides our true selves, how can we then create an environment where we feel like we can openly share our feedback and our thoughts? Creating a culture of belonging, a feeling that we can be our true selves when we come to work, is a very powerful statement. This impacts culture that impacts the individual employee. If I feel like I belong I will

have the freedom to be myself and that lends itself to providing honest, constructive feedback and ideas. If you're giving your ideas because you feel like you're in a safe space cause you belong then everyone benefits and an organization becomes more productive... I think if we strive to create an environment where people feel safe whoever they are, wherever they've come from and however they experience their life people will bring their ideas to work and in so doing bring innovation and success to the organization.

While diversity is often seen as a recruiting problem, it is actually more of a retention problem. Recruiting a diverse workforce is pointless if that workforce isn't engaged and productive. Equity, belonging and inclusion are critical parts of the overall picture, and there is a true competitive advantage for the employers who recognize and embrace this.

Solving the problem

It should be clear by now that improving diversity within an organization, especially in a way that unlocks previously unavailable pools of talent and skills, is an ongoing journey that needs to be driven by the leadership of the organization. Unfortunately, too many employers see it as a problem to solve or a special project to run. Many even think that hiring a diversity and inclusion specialist will fix things. This goes a long way to explain the gulf between the lip service paid to diversity and inclusion and the amount of actual change and improvement that is taking place. There are though many organizations that are doing some great work; while they might not have all the answers, they do represent examples of what can be done, and the positive steps employers can take. What follows is a selection of practical examples of how various employers are addressing DE&I issues and, in so doing, are benefiting by unlocking additional talent pools of digital skills.

Improving the gender balance

Frame.io is a video review and collaboration software platform based in New York City. Over the last few years, it has experienced rapid growth and very quickly scaled to over 200 people. However, as a relatively small technology company, it is facing significant recruiting challenges and competition for talent. In the words of Anna Chalon, the senior director of talent and DE&I at Frame.io:

> The New York talent market is candidate led and highly competitive. This means we have to be creative and be willing to think outside the box when it comes to our recruiting strategy. One of our strengths on the Frame.io Recruiting Team is that we move quickly and pride ourselves in providing a best-in-class candidate experience. We think it is the right thing to do for the candidate and it also allows us to hire the best talent

Diversity, equity and inclusion are mission-critical to Frame.io, and they put a massive amount of work into improving the diversity of their workforce. In a recent *Recruiting Future* podcast appearance, Anna talked through the four-step process they have followed, which she would recommend to any employer looking to put DE&I at the centre of what they do. The first step is to audit where you are currently both to understand your current employee demographic and understand how your employees are feeling. Effective change is only possible if you have a clear idea of where you are starting from. The second step is to make sure your company is building an inclusive culture. Building an inclusive culture is something that requires a large amount of thought and most definitely isn't something that employers can do overnight; however, part of Frame.io's strategy has been to focus on small practical steps. Examples include:

- Implementing training for the entire company to recognize unconscious bias.
- Making people feel safe to call out inappropriate behaviours.
- Creating employee resource groups and paying attention to details such as the naming of conference rooms and Slack channels.

The third step is hiring for diversity, and there are several actions Frame.io have taken to ensure they are fully accessing more diverse pools of talent. Questioning some unhelpful and damaging long-established beliefs that sit behind many hiring norms is critical here. For example, is having a college degree actually necessary in terms of the skills needed for the role? They are also challenging the whole concept of culture fit, focusing instead on culture 'add' to bring new perspectives and backgrounds to drive more value for the business. Looking carefully at the recruiting process itself is another important factor. Actions here include being mindful of the language used on job descriptions, particularly in an industry where gender-coded terms such as ninja or rockstar are often used. Frame.io also makes sure they have structured interviews to avoid 'gut feel' decisions and use interviewing panels that have a diverse make-up.

The fourth and final step in Frame.io's methodology is measuring and reporting on progress. This isn't just reporting for the leadership team or a small group of people; they embrace full transparency and share the reporting across the whole business. Metrics include quarterly updates on gender representation per level and yearly reports on promotions and salaries. The results of the diversity, equity and inclusion focus at Frame.io, particularly around gender balance, are impressive. Between February 2019 and July 2020, the proportion of women holding management positions increased from 19% to 47%, and during 2020 their sales team went from being 30% female to 53% female. They also increased the percentage of women in sales management positions from 20% to 54%.[19] This is even more impressive when you consider how male-dominated enterprise sales are in the technology industry.

Perhaps the standout part of Frame.io's strategy is the level of buy-in and allyship they have from the C-suite. Rachel Hirsch, one of Frame.io's recruiters, specifically spoke about this in a recent podcast interview:

> We are very lucky to have some great allies here at Frame.io, all the way up to our executive team. The one thing they do really well is that they simply show up. I actually mean that quite literally; they attend our

events and encourage other leaders to do the same. They have created
a system of accountability across the leadership team that's created a
culture where our other leaders not only feel comfortable showing up
but they feel held accountable

The gender imbalance in the technology industry cannot be solved in
isolation, and employers who join together to make a difference can
be a powerful force. An example of this type of initiative is the Talent
Tech Charter in the UK. Founded in 2017, the Talent Tech Charter is
a commitment by its signatory organizations to 'work together to
increase the inclusion and diversity of the tech workforce in the UK'.
To date, over 600 employers have signed the charter and commitment to the four key pillars of the charter.

First, 'People'; this involves having a senior signatory with their
organization who will take responsibility for the charter commitments. Second, 'Plan'; committing to develop a plan to improve
inclusion and adopt inclusive recruitment practices. Third 'Practice';
agreeing to collaborate with other signatory organizations to share
learnings both in terms of success and failures. Finally, 'Data'; contributing employee diversity data which are aggregated and anonymized
to produce an annual report and benchmarking.

The TTC has combined the learning from its signatory organization in an open playbook covering everything from building inclusive
cultures to the retention of diverse talent. In its most recent benchmarking report, the TTC found that women hold 24% of technical
roles across its signatories compared with the UK average of 16%.
One of the key drivers of this has been encouraging organizations to
have a target for the number of women on recruiting shortlists. Of
the signatories that had adopted this policy, more than half are above
the national average for the number of women in technical roles. The
Talent Tech Charter really illustrates the advantages that can be
created by employers working together even when they may be
competing with each other for talent. In the words of TTC founder
Sinead Bunting:

what's been joyful is that sometimes these kinds of collaborations
can turn into death by committees, and you have to manage different

agendas and egos. The difference with the Talent Tech Charter is that everyone cares, everyone is passionate, everyone has set aside their own individual agendas to try and collectively make a difference. This is just the start, though; we have still got so much further to go as an industry.

Reaching new pools of talent

We have already discussed the importance of inclusion and the huge benefits it brings to organizations in terms of recruiting, retention and productivity. Those employers who have a strong focus on inclusivity are also able to access additional pools of highly and often uniquely talented people. For example, one area where there has been growing awareness and action among some employers is neurodiversity. In a recent episode of the *Recruiting Future* podcast, Professor Amanda Kirby, one of the co-authors of the book *Neurodiversity at work*, gave this explanation of neurodiversity:

> So, we've all got different ways that we communicate. We've got billions of cells that are connecting in all different ways. Neurodiversity is about the differences in the way our brains work that is variable for all of us. What we're really talking about is differences of thinking and ensuring that we get the best out of people, that they can access work and show their talents. We always talk about conditions, disorders, difficulties and disabilities. When actually we should have much more of a social framing. That's where this terminology neurodiversity has come from, moving away from medical models to more social models.

The key here is the recognition that neurodivergent people can bring unique strengths to an organization. As Amanda's co-author Theo Smith says:

> People who think and act significantly different from others due to the makeup of their brain and many thousands of years of human evolution. Like people who are ADHD, Autistic, Dyslexic... often have spiky profiles... so, what does that mean? Well, they have skills in very specific areas, but it can be at the cost of other abilities. Most people, or

the 'average' brains, remain quite close across all cognitive abilities. Not veering too far from the average IQ level. But for those people who are neurodiverse, it is often recognized that their cognitive abilities can be off the chart. Either significantly above or below the average IQ level.

One example of an employer who is hugely benefiting from its understanding and inclusivity of neurodiversity is GCHQ. GCHQ has identified that those people on its apprentice scheme are four times more likely to have dyslexia than those on apprentice schemes at other organizations. This is a result of GCHQ's 'drive to recruit those whose brains process information differently. Speaking in *The Guardian*, Jo Cavan, GCHQ's director of strategy, policy and engagement, explains:[20] 'We're looking for people who can see something that's out of place in a bigger picture... .If they're sifting through large amounts of data from a large number of sources to prevent a terrorist attack or a serious organized criminal, skills such as pattern recognition are key. A lot of dyslexic colleagues have those strengths.' In order to successfully recruit and retain their neurodiverse workforce, GCHQ has had to think hard about their talent acquisition process, which is an absolutely critical lesson for other companies. They actively market themselves as a neurodiverse employer and make a number of allowances during their assessment process, such as giving extra time and allowing candidates to bring mind maps with them. They also work hard to ensure they are being inclusive in the workplace, offering managers awareness training and facilitating peer support groups. GCHQ are far from being the only employer to actively recruit neurodivergent people. For example, JP Morgan has set up a very successful Autism at Work programme. Companies such as Microsoft and SAP also have a long track record in proactively recruiting from the autism community.

There are a number of other areas where employers are breaking into new pools of talent. For example, companies such as Severn Trent Water have a substantial corporate focus on social mobility. At the same time, other organizations work collectively to support digital reskilling initiatives such as Code Clan in Scotland that brings larger pools of people into the digital workforce.

The employers doing well here have several things in common. They are challenging established institutionalized thinking within their organization about backgrounds and qualifications. They are redefining their recruiting process to be fit for purpose, and most of all, they are focusing on building inclusive workplaces to make sure everyone is happy, listened to and productive.

The way ahead

So, as we've seen, diversity, equity and inclusion isn't just about being the right thing to do for employers; it is a strategy that increases productivity, drives profitability, facilitates innovation and enables companies to tap into more pools of digital talent. However, as with any strategic initiative, there isn't a quick fix and focusing purely on tactics will not ensure positive outcomes. Big changes are needed, and companies need to work hard to help make them. Frame.io has been successful not because it has implemented unconscious bias training but because this is just one tactic in a much more significant strategic shift that has seen it get some excellent results in terms of improving gender balance. Focusing on individual tactics can actually do more harm than good. This is something that sits behind some of the questioning of the effectiveness of the unconscious bias training we have seen in recent months. Using a tool such as a one-off training session in isolation without a broader strategy will not get the results employers need. The same is also true with technology. While technology has a massive role to play in diversity, equity and inclusion, as we will explore further in the next chapter, it is not a silver bullet here and can actually have some significant negative implications. The other aspect of DE&I strategies is that there are no quick fixes and long-term thinking is absolutely essential. For example, global security and airspace company Lockheed Martin has a strategy for attracting diverse talent that clearly illustrates this.[21] They have a talent engagement approach that sees it communicating with a potential hire over a three to eight-year lifecycle before recruiting them. This allows them to reach out to pools of diverse talent while they are still at school, with ongoing inspiration and support that helps communities and at the same time enhances Lockheed Martin's employer brand with those communities.

Ultimately it is the leadership of companies that need to take both responsibility and accountability here. We saw early in the chapter that although leadership attitudes have shifted in the last 18 months, there is still very little measurable board-level accountability for diversity, equity and inclusion. This means that progress remains slow.

There is a real opportunity for competitive advantage, and it is something all CEOs should be taking action on. One example of a CEO putting DE&I front and centre is Jerome Ternynck from talent acquisition technology company SmartRecruiters. In 2020 Jerome made a public commitment to being 'an anti-racist force in the recruiting market' and acknowledged that their first step in doing this was for the organization he leads to be a role model. In October 2020, SmartRecruiters publicly published a list of 10 principles of diversity hiring[22] to drive the debate in the industry. These principles were: diverse hiring teams, awareness training, clear representation objectives, inclusive hiring process, neutral description, dedicated sourcing, no bias screening, structured interviewing, inclusive onboarding and fair internal hiring. Many of these are practices already embedded in the employers used as case studies and examples in this chapter.

The employer and employees win when the C-suite lead the way and make themselves accountable. The benefits and the imperative are clear. The companies who get this right and build successful DE&I strategies will have a digital talent advantage over their competition.

Chapter summary

Diverse organizations have a huge competitive advantage and are able to access bigger pools of digital talent. However, improving diversity is a long-term challenge that is centred on building an inclusive culture. Bias is systemic and leadership and accountability from the C-suite is a critical part of building more diverse organizations. As we have explored in this chapter:

- Though diverse workforces offer a huge competitive advantage, it is still not a priority for most organizations
- Better diversity cannot be achieved without building an inclusive culture
- Diversity hiring offers the opportunity to tap into broader pools of digital talent
- Seeking 'Culture fit' hardwires bias and harms cognitive diversity
- Recruiting processes must be inclusive and demonstrate allyship and accountability from the company's leadership.

Endnotes

1 Avado. Mind the Gap, cdn2.hubspot.net/hubfs/511436/1-Pagers/Mind%20 The%20Gap%20One%20Pager%20w%20CTA.pdf (archived at https://perma. cc/PV9P-XDDY)

2 HR Tech Conference. CHRO Series Part 1 – Diversity and Inclusion: What Practices Work?', Human Resource Executive, hrexecutive.com/chro-series-part-1-diversity-and-inclusion-what-practices-work/

3 M Silverthorn (2020) *Authentic Diversity: How to change the workplace for good*, Routledge, London

4 V Hunt, D Layton and S Prince, Why Diversity Matters, 1 January 2015. www. mckinsey.com/business-functions/organization/our-insights/why-diversity-matters (archived at https://perma.cc/28CV-Y4YA)

5 V Hunt, L Yee, S Prince and S Dixon-Fyle. Delivering through Diversity, 18 January 2018. www.mckinsey.com/business-functions/organization/our-insights/ delivering-through-diversity (archived at https://perma.cc/P6CD-Y98F)

6 R Lorenzo, N Voigt, K Schetelig, A Zawadzki, I Welpe, and P Brosi. The Mix that Matters, 26 April 2017. www.bcg.com/publications/2017/people-organization-leadership-talent-innovation-through-diversity-mix-that-matters (archived at https://perma.cc/7SHY-U4JX)

7 Accenture. Getting to Equal: The Disability Inclusion Advantage, www. accenture.com/_acnmedia/pdf-89/accenture-disability-inclusion-research-report.pdf (archived at https://perma.cc/2ZAV-ZYJK)

8 A Thalheim. Researchers Find 'Diversity Disaster' in Artificial Intelligence Industry, Washington Square News, 22 April 2019. nyunews.com/news/2019/04/22/nyu-ai-institute-study-artificial-intelligence-discrimination/ (archived at https://perma.cc/C6KG-SP75)

9 J Dastin. Amazon scraps secret AI recruiting tool that showed bias against women, Reuters, 11 October 2018. www.reuters.com/article/us-amazon-com-jobs-automation-insight/amazon-scraps-secret-ai-recruiting-tool-that-showed-bias-against-women-idUSKCN1MK08G (archived at https://perma.cc/UQN2-BDMR)

10 JCQ Examination Results, www.jcq.org.uk/examination-results/?post-year=2020 (archived at https://perma.cc/XG8Q-UVCS)

11 E Spelke. Sex Differences in Intrinsic Aptitude for Mathematics and Science?: A Critical Review, *American Psychologist*, 2006, January 60(9), www.researchgate.net/publication/7403682_Sex_Differences_in_Intrinsic_Aptitude_for_Mathematics_and_Science_A_Critical_Review (archived at https://perma.cc/DD4K-5D4S)

12 OECD. What Lies Behind Gender Inequality in Education?, PISA in Focus, No. 49. www.oecd-ilibrary.org/education/what-lies-behind-gender-inequality-in-education_5js4xffhhc30-en (archived at https://perma.cc/CS3C-VJAS)

13 R Navarro. Unconscious Bias, University of California, San Francisco, https://diversity.ucsf.edu/resources/unconscious-bias (archived at https://perma.cc/Z6VT-W9QF)

14 M Alder. Recruiting Future. Ep 341: Culture Fit Doesn't Exist (podcast) 31 March 2021. recruitingfuture.com/2021/03/ep-341-culture-fit-doesnt-exist/ (archived at https://perma.cc/6F26-3DED)

15 K Wheeler. Is culture fit an excuse to be biased, LinkedIn, 31 May 2019. www.linkedin.com/pulse/culture-fit-excuse-biased-kevin-wheeler/ (archived at https://perma.cc/89JE-NF2V)

16 A Hern. Twitter apologises for 'racist' image-cropping algorithm, *The Guardian*, 21 September 2020. www.theguardian.com/technology/2020/sep/21/twitter-apologises-for-racist-image-cropping-algorithm (archived at https://perma.cc/B2B5-BMHY)

17 CIPD. Building Inclusive Workplaces, 23 September 2019. www.cipd.co.uk/knowledge/fundamentals/relations/diversity/building-inclusive-workplaces (archived at https://perma.cc/J66C-ND2W)

18 M Alder. *Recruiting Future*. Ep 203: Diversity, Inclusion, Equity & Belonging (podcast) 16 August 2019. recruitingfuture.com/2019/08/ep-203-diversity-inclusion-equity-belonging/ (archived at https://perma.cc/GLG9-T69J)

19 M Alder. *Recruiting Future*. Ep 249: Delivering A Custom Experience (podcast) 17 March 2020. recruitingfuture.com/2020/03/ep-249-delivering-a-custom-experience/ (archived at https://perma.cc/E96F-8P3W)

20 R Hall. People with dyslexia have skills that we need, says GCHQ, *The Guardian*, 29 April 2021. www.theguardian.com/uk-news/2021/apr/29/people-with-dyslexia-have-skills-that-we-need-says-gchq (archived at https://perma.cc/8Y5X-QNAP)

21 M Alder. *Recruiting Future*. Ep 356: Talent Engagement (podcast) 26 May 2021. recruitingfuture.com/2021/05/ep-356-talent-engagement/ (archived at https://perma.cc/LB49-RHXC)

22 J Ternyck. The 10 Principles of Diversity Hiring, LinkedIn, 14 October 2020. www.linkedin.com/pulse/10-principles-diversity-hiring-jerome-ternynck/ (archived at https://perma.cc/5MQU-ZFXJ)

07

Work Tech

From HR tech to Work Tech

Over the last 20 years, the digital revolution has changed our expectations of the world. Whether it is shopping, travel, health, fitness or a myriad of other daily activities, we expect connection, instant service, rock-solid availability and transparent communication. This growth in expectations is also speeding up. A one-week delivery time for e-commerce seemed incredible 20 years ago; it would be an unacceptable inconvenience now with next day delivery as standard and next hour delivery starting to come on stream in larger cities.

Expectations in our work-life absolutely mirror those in the rest of our lives, but unfortunately, the systems and software used in our working lives do not always measure up. Traditional corporate technology has struggled to keep pace with the rapid acceleration in the development of consumer technology, particularly in terms of intuitive interfaces and overall user experience. The implications for companies are profound.

Early in 2021, technology company Dell teamed up with neurological research company Emotiv to conduct a unique piece of research that used a brain scanner to explore the effect technology has on workplace productivity and well-being.[1] The results were pretty conclusive. Using bad technology (in this case, software that is difficult to use or suffers all too common failures) doubles workplace stress. It has a cumulative and sustained effect with implications for productivity and well-being. This was seen to be the case among younger digitally native age groups particularly. Conversely, the research also showed that using good technology, i.e. software that works effectively, had a positive brain impact and increased workplace productivity by a massive 43%.

As we have seen, digital transformation is driving the need for digital talent within organizations; human resources must go through its own digital transformation to have culture, ways of working, processes, tools and technologies that are fit for purpose to support the transforming organization.

Effective workplace technology is a critical element of an effective digital transformation. This is something that was true before COVID-19 and is absolutely paramount as we move forward. Businesses are having to evolve and transform quickly. It makes no sense to spend vast amounts of time and resources attracting or developing digital skills if you don't then give people the systems and tools they need to be as productive as possible that also helps enhance well-being within the employee experience.

HR technology also plays a critical role in developing and acquiring digital skills. Advances in talent acquisition, talent management and learning and development technologies offer the opportunity for companies to recruit, retain and develop talent faster and more effectively than ever before.

In Chapter 1, we talked about how HR technology has changed over the last 10 years to support different people priorities and ways of working, moving from a system of record to a system of engagement and interaction. However, changes in technology are meaningless if they are not part of the overall change within a business and are supported by the right processes and the right mindset. For those employers who were lagging behind in their thinking, 2020 was probably the biggest wake-up call they could possibly get.

The COVID-19 pandemic has been transformational in terms of the relationship between technology and work. At the beginning of 2020, a vast number of the world's knowledge workers were forced to leave their offices at short notice as employers were forced into the immediate adoption of the work from home model. HR technology took on a whole new importance with the words Zoom and Teams falling into everyday use as the world strived to continue as far as possible with business as usual, albeit, for many, in a virtual format. As we will see consistently through this chapter, the imposition of technology-based working for knowledge workers has exponentially increased the importance of HR technology and dramatically accelerated its adoption cycle.

For many organizations, the early months of 2020 were the first time they had even considered the possibility that their organization could operate with a remote workforce, and indeed could continue to do so for an extended period of time, and perhaps in many cases, permanently. The impact of the adoption of HR technology was seismic. Old arguments and objections fell away as companies scrambled to get up and running with new technologies or quickly adapt existing software for use in ways that had never been considered before to support their employees who were having to find makeshift workspaces in their homes.

One of the lessons we all quickly learned from the pandemic was just how much of our previously face-to-face, in-person lives could be conducted remotely over video. Family get-togethers, work nights out, trips to the theatre, exercise classes; the level of creativity people used to try and replicate their lives online seemed to know no bounds. What was happening in people's personal lives was very much being mirrored at work. Recruiting, onboarding, learning and development, talent management and many other vital people activities had to adapt to the remote environment, something that was particularly challenging as they are all areas that have relied on face-to-face contact in the past.

The steps taken by employers during 2020 and 2021 were reflex reactions to an unprecedented emergency, in many cases without any contingency plans or forward thinking to fall back on and very often supported by technology that was not actually fit for purpose. For example, Microsoft Teams, Zoom and their equivalents were never designed to be robust interviewing or learning platforms. While they offered a temporary medium-term solution, as we will see, employers are exploring or adopting specialist software to solve their challenges in the longer term. As we move to the next stage of 'the new world of work', whether companies choose to stay remote, get everyone back to the office or try and find a balance between the two (more on this in the next chapter), there are lessons to learn and new ways of thinking about technology to drive productivity and accelerate the digital transformation.

The level of venture capital being invested into HR technology had already been growing massively in the years leading up to the COVID-19 pandemic. According to data collated by HR Technology analyst George LaRocque from WorkTech, over $5 billion was invested in areas including Core HR, payroll, wellness, L&D, talent management, internal communication and talent acquisition during 2019. Understandably this fell back a bit during 2020, but even then, overall investment still came close to the $5 billion mark.

The increased focus on HR technology driven by COVID-19 has led to investment reaching unprecedented heights in 2021. $7.62 billion was invested in just the first half of 2021, more money than was invested in the whole of 2019. In Q2 alone, there were 17 'mega-deal' investments to the value of $100 million or more going to individual companies. This level of sustained investment has also birthed multiple 'unicorns', software vendors with valuations of over $1 billion, as well as entirely new subcategories of technology (more on this later).

Investment at this level signals that there is a huge amount of confidence in the future of HR technology. It also translates into the kind of budgets for product development, developing marketing narratives and customer acquisition that will actually shape the future of work. In early 2021, Global HR analyst and influencer, Josh Bersin used his annual *HR Technology Marketplace*[2] report to focus on just how much COVID-19 has been a game-changer for the sector. With a renewed focus on the employee experience and productivity, Bersin suggested that rather than the software being labelled as HR tech, the name 'Work Tech' would better reflect the changes taking place. The phrase Work Tech is now being widely adopted, and that is what we will be using for the rest of the chapter.

Although marketing hype fuels headlines and builds excitement among investors, it is critical that we look at Work Tech through a practical lens. What are employers finding useful, what barriers to adoption remain and how do HR leaders build and execute effective strategies at a time of such intense disruption and reinvention to the world of work?

In the rest of this chapter, we will work to cut through the hype and look pragmatically at the implications of the Work Tech revolution in terms of digital talent. We will identify the opportunities employers now have at their disposal and the actions that need to be taken to realize the immense potential that Work Tech offers.

Technology trends

The world of work is getting more complex and, as we have discussed, ever more reliant on technology. As key technology trigger points have emerged over the last 20 years, they have a corresponding impact on talent acquisition, management and development. So, 20 years ago, it was the arrival of the internet to the mass market; 10 years later, social media and smartphones changed the way we communicate. At the same time, cloud computing changed how HR technology worked to speed up implementation, drive adoption and accelerate product development. As we move into 2022 and beyond, recent innovations in AI, automation and the application of data science are defining another new era of even more radical change.

With complexity, though, comes noise and confusion. It can be challenging to take a helicopter view to get a real sense of what is going on and how to navigate these highly disruptive times. One way to see the wood for the trees is to identify and understand the key trends that are driving the current explosion in this new era of Work Tech growth. As previously mentioned, AI, automation and data are the critical components here and are also profoundly interrelated. Let's look at each of them in a bit more detail.

AI

AI has been the biggest buzzword in Work Tech for several years. Almost every Work Tech vendor now has AI deeply embedded in their solutions. AI comes up time and time again whenever HR and talent acquisition professionals are surveyed about their current priorities.

However, when you dig beneath the surface, there is minimal consensus about what AI means and a tremendous amount of confusion. This seems to be as true for suppliers as it is for practitioners, making software purchasing decisions even harder as benchmarking and like for like comparisons can often be impossible.

Artificial Intelligence is, in reality, a very broad term with an ever-changing definition. In the most general terms, it describes a machine process that replicates the intellectual capacity of a human. The key elements that we have seen in Work Tech over the last few years are algorithms, machine learning, natural language processing and deep learning.

- An algorithm, in its simplest terms is just a set of rules for carrying out a task.

- Machine learning refers to the ability of computer systems to combine complex algorithms and statistical models to adapt and learn from analysing patterns in data.

- Developments in combining natural language processing with deep learning technologies entered the mainstream from around 2014. Their rapid evolution has led to a giant leap forward in what is now possible from AI. Natural language processing (NLP) is the term that describes a computer's ability to understand human language as it is spoken or written.

- Deep learning is a function of AI that imitates the workings of the human brain, drawing on unstructured data to recognize patterns and make decisions.

However, even with the ever-increasing sophistication of AI, it currently falls a long way short of some of the expectations loaded onto it. We are still very much in the era of artificial narrow intelligence, where AI is still designed to complete very specific and often very specialized tasks. The age of artificial general intelligence, where it is predicted that AI will have the same intellectual capacity as a human, isn't likely to be technically possible for at least another 20 years.

The lack of transparency from some vendors about the type of technology they are using, and the potential limitations of its capabilities has led to accusations of marketing spin. This is undoubt-edly the case when 'AI-driven' solutions are offered as silver bullets to solve problems such as hiring diversity. It is also part of the overall picture, but competitive confidentiality and a lack of understanding from buyers are also vital factors here.

Differentiation is a big issue, however. Megan Butler, a leading expert on AI in HR, highlighted the problem back in 2019, speaking on the *Recruiting Future* podcast:[3]

> A lot of what we are seeing are traditional processes that just have some smart tech layered on top, but you can't really traditionally classify it as AI. There are also a lot of companies doing very cool things that are using AI and have game-changer ideas; they tend to have a lot more challenges because they're doing something different.

Megan also identified talent acquisition as the most significant growth area for AI. Various types of matching algorithms are being used in different ways in an attempt to make recruiting smarter and more efficient:

> They're helping talent acquisition to have more data points to make better decisions. It is not a zero-sum game where it's either a recruiter making the decision or the AI making a decision, but it's a mix and augmentation where recruiters are able to use a wider set of information, including their own experiences with the candidate, what they've seen in an interview plus and what they've seen through an assessment tool to improve decision-making process.

As we will see later in the chapter, this type of intelligent, machine augmented matching is also becoming a crucial part of talent manage-ment, learning and development and internal mobility.

Access to large data sets is crucial for the success of AI. Here Jon Krohn, the chief data scientist at Nebula, outlines the process under-taken to build a system that predicts the probability of a job applicant being invited to interview:

> We have hundreds of millions of training data points that we've accumulated over the years of particular people with particular

resumes being invited to interview or being not invited to interview for particular jobs. So, each of those hundreds of millions of cases, we have a resume, we have a job description, and we have the outcome that we'd like to predict. We have a yes or a no as to whether that particular person was invited to the job, or they weren't invited to the job. So by training the machine learning model on hundreds of millions of cases like that, it can build up a really nuanced and complex understanding of the kinds of people that are an appropriate fit for a particular job.[4]

The reliance on such massive datasets for success raises essential questions about bias and ethics when AI is being used both as a tool to assist decision making and, in some instances, as a tool to automate decision making. Ultimately AI can only deal with the data it has and has no context for where the data comes from and the manner in which it was collected. The widely reported large technology company example mentioned in the previous chapter, where an AI tool automatically screened out women, is a strong example of the dangers here. The data used to train the system were already systemically biased toward male candidates and AI just amplified this. This kind of algorithmic bias isn't just an issue for large tech companies who can develop their own systems; it is potentially a problem for any employer who is using a vendor with an AI element in their product. With the vast prevalence of AI in the Work Tech products in the market, this kind of bias is a potential problem for many employers and a key consideration for many others who are considering implementing AI solutions in the next few years.

At the end of 2018, Upturn, a US-based think tank non-profit with a mission to promote equity and justice in the design and use of digital technology, published a research paper entitled *Help Wanted: An Examination of Hiring Algorithms, Equity and Bias*.[5] The report is the first study of its kind and examines how predictive recruiting tools affect equity through the hiring process.

The report recognized that technology wasn't making the final decision about who got hired but was playing a role in who got rejected, which job advertisements were seen by which job seeker and influencing other areas such as salary and prediction of likely job performance.

It also identified that predictive hiring tools have the potential to amplify institutional and systemic bias. What is interesting here is that removing specific identifying information from CVs and job applications was no defence against this: 'Predictions based on past hiring decisions and evaluations can both reveal and reproduce patterns of inequity at all stages of the hiring process, even when tools explicitly ignore race, gender, age, and other protected attributes.'

Upturn also raised an important point about the interaction between recruiters and predictive hiring tools. One of the significant defences about the use of AI in talent acquisition is that it is not designed (currently anyway) to replace recruiters, it is just there to provide additional data points to help them make a fully informed decision. Upturn identified that hiring tools that score or rank job applicants may be overstating marginal distinctions between candidates. The level to which these ranking influences recruiters' decisions is still unknown, but the potential for hidden bias to drive hiring decisions is significant. There is, however, a flip side to all of this, and if deployed, managed and measured in the right way, then AI recruiting tools can be used to reduce bias and improve diversity in hiring. In their research, Upturn acknowledged that new hiring technologies could 'improve the poor baseline' of dealing with bias against women, people of colour and underrepresented groups.

In a recent interview on the *Recruiting Future* podcast, Mahe Bayireddi, CEO and co-founder of Phenom, an AI-powered talent experience management (TXM) platform, talked about the role that technology can play in improving diversity and identifying bias:

> The recruitment process has a lot of bias because humans all have a bias that they carry with them ... This is where we need to create more awareness and more transparency. Diversity & Inclusion is not an AI problem – it's not created by AI and it can't be solved by AI. AI helps by bringing awareness to what's happening by creating a clear documentation of the bias that exists in the hiring process.[6]

This is a powerful argument for AI as a force for good in uncovering previously hidden patterns of bias and arming companies with the data and intelligence to be better. It's clear that AI is here to stay, and its role and influence in Work Tech will only continue to grow over the coming years. It is essential then that those buyers understand what they are purchasing and the advantages and risk factors of AI-driven solutions.

Upturn recommends that vendors are dramatically more transparent about the predictive tools they build and allow independent auditing. Transparency is critical in mitigating the dangers of decisions that AI influences by fully understanding the data and algorithms being used to drive its outputs. This principle applies not just to the talent acquisition examples we have seen where AI is more advanced, but also to other areas in HR. AI is increasingly being used to drive decision making in talent management, L&D and internal mobility, so getting the operating principles right at this early stage is incredibly important.

One vendor taking this call for transparency in AI very seriously is the talent acquisition tool, Predictive Hire. They recently developed the Fair AI for Recruitment framework (FAIR): a set of measures and guidelines to implement and maintain fairness in AI-based candidate selection tools. The framework won a Cogx award for Best Innovation in Algorithmic Bias Mitigation in 2021. It has four properties: inclusive, unbiased, explainable and valid. 'Inclusive' is all about ensuring that all candidates are treated equally when going through an AI-driven process. The example used is the fairness of timed tests for candidates with cognitive disabilities. The framework recognized that this is the property that it is most difficult for vendors to demonstrate as there may be some subjectivity around the notion of equal treatment. 'Unbiased' is making sure that AI is not showing bias towards any group defined by a protective attribute. There are a number of bias testing toolkits that already exist in the market that can test for this. 'Explainable' is providing documentation and tools to help to make sense of the outcomes of the AI solution. Predictive Hire sees this working on several levels, explaining the science behind the predictive models and also providing explanations for individual outcomes by giving candidates and hiring managers the insights to do this. 'Valid' concerns demonstrating the validity of the predictions of the AI and how accurately it predicts the outcome it is supposed to.

Ultimately the key here is transparency. Vendors need to be transparent about how their AI works, but employers also need to be asking them the right questions. AI will provide enormous benefits, but there are also huge risks if buyers don't go into the purchasing process with their eyes wide open.

Data and analytics

Data and analytics are playing an increasingly important role in HR and people operations. 'People analytics' has been attracting a growing amount of interest as a topic for many years now, and as such, it is a very well documented trend. With so many great books and articles already written on people analytics, we don't want to cover too much of the same ground here. However, there are some specific aspects of the growing importance of data-driven decision making that make it a key trend in the acquisition, retention and development of digital talent. Data plays an absolutely pivotal role, both in the development of AI and also in the automation of many HR and talent acquisition processes. Therefore, employers must view it as a critically important trend that they understand when building a Work Tech strategy.

Let's start by looking at a few definitions. The CIPD describes people analytics as 'analysing data about people to solve business problems'.[7] It can be used in a wide variety of settings, including talent acquisition, learning and development and employee engagement to make decisions, improve performance and illustrate impact.

People analytics (and indeed any kind of data analytics) broadly works at three levels which the CIPD links to the maturity level of the people analytics' function within an organization: the first level is descriptive analytics, which looks at historical data to explore trends or particular snapshots over time to make better decisions. This can be achieved by looking specifically at one source of data or combining different types and sources of data. The second level is predictive analytics, which is taking historical data to build models and predict future trends. Finally, the third level is prescriptive analytics, which uses the outputs of descriptive and predictive analytics to automate recommendations and decision making.

The CIPD reports that while many organizations are capable of producing effective descriptive analytics, relatively few are able to work at the predictive people analytics' level. However, the growth of Work Tech solutions that have predictive and prescriptive analytics rolled into their solutions means that the advantages of operating at these levels are open to many more employers. There are also tools in the market that aggregate data across disparate data platforms and sources to provide people analytics' insights. For example, in August 2021, software giant SAP acquired Scooptalent, 'a platform powered by natural language processing, AI and machine learning that combines, analyses and trains data from disparate human resource systems and workflows'.[8]

At the same time, Work Tech is extensively increasing the amount of data available as software is being used to drive more HR and talent acquisition areas than ever before. We have particularly seen this during the pandemic, with employers being forced to use technology in new and more creative ways. We are also now witnessing a systematization of technology in key areas of the talent ecosystem, which is increasing the number of data points available and giving employers access to increasingly deeper insights. We looked at the way technology is revolutionizing talent management and learning and development in Chapter 4. Here are some examples of this in action in talent acquisition.

1 Corporate careers sites have always played a key role in recruitment marketing but have traditionally been built in a static way that doesn't harness the full sophistication of digital marketing. In recent years career site systems have come onto the market offering a true digital marketing platform for talent attraction. Career site system vendors such as Attrax offer employers the ability to optimize careers' site content based on real-time audience behaviour, offering a personalized experience that helps their employers stand out in crowded talent markets. They collect data on candidate preferences and behaviour that provides insights that are helping to revolutionize recruitment marketing.

2 During the COVID-19 pandemic, video interviewing moved into the mainstream of talent acquisition. Lockdowns and remote working meant talent acquisition teams were forced to move to virtual recruiting and video interviewing platforms which saw hyper-growth. Video interviewing offers many advantages, and one of these is the fact that interviews can now be recorded at scale and assessed for consistency, quality and bias. This, in turn, has seen the growth of 'interview intelligence' platforms such as Metaview. Using natural language processing and AI, companies like Metaview analyse the content of video and audio interviews to provide unique data, analytics and actionable feedback to help interviewers improve.

3 Candidate experience has always been an enormous issue in talent acquisition, and it has traditionally been seen as an awareness, resource and education problem with employers. Technology is now enabling the use of data to make the candidate experience a science, something that can be personalized and optimized in real-time. Assessment provider SHL offers a great example of where data can be used to scientifically improve the candidate experience. On average, half a million candidates a week are assessed on SHL's digital platform. SHL synthesizes hundreds of data points during a single candidate's experience using machine learning and advanced analytics. This drives insights that can power an agile approach to candidate experience, for example, offering the ability to do A / B testing on recruiting workflows and content.[9]

Although data and analytics have been a focus in HR and talent acquisition for a while, it still feels that we are in the very early days of realizing the potential they offer to strategically help attract, retain and develop digital talent for organizations. This is a fast-developing trend, and HR and talent acquisition teams must be firmly focused on improving data literacy, particularly when it comes to understanding the new data points that analytics Work Tech are making available. There is a real challenge here, with research by the Data Literacy Project[10] revealing that 93% of business decision-makers believe that it is important for employees to be data literate, but only 24% of the global workforce feel fully confident in their ability to work with data. Where there is a challenge, though, there is always an opportunity as the same research indicates that 78% of the global workforce is willing to invest time and energy into improving their data skills. With only 17% of companies 'significantly encouraging' employees to be more comfortable with data, the route to a competitive advantage here is a clear one.

Automation

The three trends we are looking at are deeply interrelated but also have their own distinct nuances. Automation is essentially powered by AI and driven by data but also has its own set of challenges and considerations. Automation isn't just a growing trend; it is the inevitable conclusion for a large amount of the communication, interaction and processes within the talent lifecycle. Businesses have been moving further towards automation for years, and rapid developments in technology and the impact of the pandemic have rapidly accelerated this. In their 2020 report *The Future of Jobs*, the World Economic Forum indicated that 80% of the business leaders they surveyed during the pandemic intended to accelerate the automation of their work processes.[11]

While many business processes and customer interactions have already been automated, there has historically been a reluctance among HR and talent acquisition professionals to embrace or, in some cases, even to discuss automation. The thinking has often been that such people-centric functions cannot be automated because they rely so much on human-to-human interaction. An algorithm can't find the right emotional resonance to persuade someone to change jobs, and a robot does not have the empathy required to have a difficult performance conversation.

However, what has become clear is that the robots vs humans discourse that has characterized conversations about automation is wide of the mark. The reality of the situation is much more nuanced. As we have already seen, AI, machine learning and predictive analytics offer the potential for humans to make better decisions. Talent acquisition can also be highly inefficient, and HR is full of repeatable processes. These are the perfect conditions for automation, and when you add in the drive from the C-suite towards automated business processes, automation is inescapable. The key point to make here is that automation isn't just about driving efficiencies and improving the bottom line. Automation can make things possible that were not possible before, and it can radically improve the candidate and employee experience. Numerous positive case studies are emerging, and talent acquisition and HR professionals must educate themselves and drive the automation strategy to achieve the best possible people outcomes. This is a huge opportunity. So, what can be automated? The mantra has always been that automation in the talent lifecycle works best with simple repeatable tasks. This is undoubtedly true, but we are now seeing much more sophistication in automation, taking things to another level. As always seems to be the case with technology adoption, talent acquisition is leading the way, but automation is now starting to happen across the talent lifecycle. Here are just a few examples of where we are already seeing automation working in practice: sourcing, recruitment marketing, interview scheduling, candidate screening, onboarding, objective setting, coaching, engagement monitoring and elements of outplacement. It is imperative to note that there is still a significant human element in all of these processes. Automation is enabling people to work smarter; it is not completely replacing them. There are also three types of automation at work in these activities: process, matching and conversational. Although there is much crossover here, it does help to look at them individually.

Process automation is driven by the rise of robotic process automation (RPA), which first really took hold in finance departments. Most large companies are now looking for efficiencies by automating mundane rules-based processes. CIO.com describes RPA as using technology and business logic to create a robot, 'to capture and interpret applications for processing a transaction, manipulating data, triggering responses and communicating with other digital systems. RPA scenarios range from something as simple as generating an automatic response to an email to deploying thousands of bots, each programmed to automate jobs in an ERP system.'[12]

The second type of automation we are seeing deployed in the talent lifecycle is matching automation, something we have already discussed in the context of the AI that drives it. This is the area that needs the greatest amount of monitoring, transparency and human intervention to ensure fairness and that systemic bias is not embedded and amplified by the AI involved. The third and perhaps most significant type of automation from the perspective of people-centric functions is conversational automation. The rise of chatbots in talent acquisition and HR has been a rapid one, even before the COVID-19 pandemic. The initial scepticism around making candidates and employees speak to robots is starting to subside as the advantages become clearer. Rather than damaging the candidate or employee experience, chatbots are in some cases dramatically enhancing it by offering a 24-hour service, straightforward communication and easy access to information. We are also seeing rapid advances in sophistication with simple scripted chatbots evolving in fully conversational AI and managing ever more complex communication scenarios.

With automation set to continue to be one of the biggest trends in HR and talent acquisition for years to come, it is vitally important that employers have the proper strategic foundation in place to build on moving forward. Several elements need to be considered.

First, there are data, bias and analytics issues that we have discussed several times already in this chapter. It is critical that automated processes actually do make things more efficient and don't cause unintended consequences such as amplifying bias. Data and analytics critically underpin automation and help people leaders to understand exactly what they need to automate and optimize the results they are getting. Developing a robust approach to data and analytics is a critical part of an effective automation strategy. Second, and perhaps most importantly, is finding the right balance between automation and human interaction. Where does automation add value, and where is it critical that human touchpoints are maintained? As we have already seen, a growing familiarity with chatbots and appreciation for their convenience means that automated communication is preferred by many when it comes to the more transactional aspects of communication in recruiting and HR processes. This would have been unthinkable a few years ago and illustrates that it is often difficult to predict precisely where the split between human and machine should be. At this early stage in their automation journeys, employers need to focus on implementing a hybrid model and continually experiment with human and automated communication touchpoints. It is likely that the optimal mix will also vary from industry to industry and organization to organization. The third element is content and messaging. One of the most common mistakes we see with automation is that employers focus purely on the technology and do not consider the actual message they want to get across to their audiences. Empathetic communication is critical both internally and externally. In talent acquisition, employers should also seek the kind of emotional connection recruiters need to get the attention of potential hires, develop an interest in a job role through persuasion and then convert that interest into a successful application. Without a detailed content plan, there is a danger that automated communication just becomes large scale spamming that alienates everyone.

Pragmatism and adoption

As we have seen, the hype around Work Tech is off the scale due to changing approaches to work driven by the pandemic and a marketing machine driven by billions of dollars of venture capital investment. The amount of noise created in the market by vendors, commentators and analysts can make it very difficult to see the woods for the trees. Often, people leaders feel that they are a long way behind their peers regarding Work Tech implementation and adoption. The reality of the situation is actually very different. With so much disruption happening in the market, there are very, very few employers who are 100% comfortable with their technology strategies. Even those employers who are held up as bastions of best practice in particular areas will undoubtedly be struggling in others.

It is important to acknowledge that employers can reach no fixed endpoint when it comes to Work Tech. Technology is now such a fundamental element of the talent functions within employment that it has to be addressed with an ever-evolving strategic response rather than as a one-off project or procurement issue. Before the pandemic, it might have been fair to say that innovation in Work Tech was almost unsustainably behind the actual adoption of technology. There was a sense that even with the pressures of corporate digital transformation, HR and talent acquisition teams could take their time developing strategies without losing competitive advantage.

We often talk about the revolutionary changes that technology has made in people functions. In reality, change has previously always been more of a slow fade than an abrupt jump cut. HR has always been risk-averse when it comes to developments in technology. It took several years for changes driven by technological innovations such as cloud computing, the mobile internet and social media to filter through into HR processes and talent acquisition methodologies. Although the pace of adoption has historically been slow, the rate of innovation has continued to speed up. With such giant leaps forward, it is not unsurprising that many employers have struggled to keep pace.

The pandemic has changed everything, and the digital skills crisis is now pressingly urgent. Work Tech is a critical part of the solution offering the potential to increase the sophistication of talent acquisition, improve the employee experience, turbocharge skills development and power a considerable growth in internal mobility. As we will see shortly, a strategic approach to technology is critical here, but that isn't possible without a mindset shift and a substantial focus on the importance of digital literacy. If HR and talent acquisition teams want to stay relevant and have a strong voice inside their organizations, it is vital that they educate themselves on the current trends in the technology market, the current art of the possible and the future possibilities that Work Tech offers.

It is great to see the importance of digital literacy now being reflected in the vocational education of the next generation of HR leaders, with universities adapting their courses to the new realities facing the professional. The University of Kingston is an excellent example with Lisa Henderson, Course Director of the MSc in Global HRM, sharing these thoughts on their approach.

> The role of HR is changing at speed and with it comes skills that have never been used by HR – it is not enough to be a 'people person' anymore. To really thrive and deliver the best for our workforces, there is a need for HR professionals to be brave, dive into technology and embrace the opportunities it can provide. Digital literacy is key to providing robust business cases, attraction and retention of talent and give a stronger connection to people in organisations today.

Strategy

With so much innovation going on in Work Tech and an ever-growing number of new user cases, having a solid strategy in place is critical. We have seen that the speed of technology adoption in HR is an issue. Conversely, there can also be a tendency towards shiny objects and silver bullet syndrome with employers purchasing technology on the promise that it will solve urgent challenges or just to try and create the perception of innovation. Most of the time, this kind of approach fails to deliver either of these things! Long-term strategic thinking is critical here and is something that should be driven by business needs and objectives rather than short-term tactics or the noise of vendor marketing spin.

The Work Tech market is confusing, even for those with a high degree of digital literacy. HR and talent acquisition teams also have internal complications with IT and procurement that may limit their choices and abilities to purchase technology. One of the more dominant trends of the last decade has been employers implementing software suites for all their business processes, from single enterprise vendors, such as Oracle, to SAP and Workday. While this can bring considerable advantages in terms of efficiency and consistency of data, it is also very limiting for areas of the business such as talent acquisition who would benefit from using specialist solutions (often referred to as point solutions). Fast-changing talent markets need a dynamic and agile approach. A dedicated recruiting system is likely to be more flexible than a system that is also providing payroll and core HR services.

The suite versus point solution issue has got even more challenging in the last few years as high levels of investment have enabled vendors to expand their offerings in other areas of the talent lifecycle. Examples include former L&D platforms offering talent and performance management solutions and former ATS (Applicant Tracker Systems) vendors branching out into onboarding and internal mobility.

As we have seen throughout the book, the acquisition, development and retention of talent is an issue that is finally getting the attention of the C-suite. Hopefully, this will lead to more flexible thinking when it comes to company-wide enterprise software decisions. This makes it even more important that HR and talent acquisition leaders are clear on technology strategies that will drive compelling business cases.

So, what are the critical elements of an effective Work Tech strategy? Every market is different, and every employer has its own unique circumstances; however, they are some fundamentals that should be in every strategic blueprint.

- **Objectives:** What are you looking to achieve with technology, and how does this reflect back to overall company objectives. What context are you seeking to match a solution to?

- **Ongoing Research:** This is a continuous process of education on the Work Tech market, the current art of the possible and likely future trends. In such a dynamic and disruptive market, it is vital that research is always ongoing in the background rather than just being a stage of a specific project.

- **Analysis:** Keep asking the following questions to understand your current position and what you need moving forward. What are the limitations of your existing software (if applicable), and what value are you getting from it? What kind of experience do your users expect? What corporate constraints current exist around technology procurement? How can business cases be built to challenge them?

- **Selection & Implementation:** The world is moving quickly, and you need to as well. Can you pilot and test solutions? How can the decision-making process be quicker and more agile but also robust enough to reduce risk? How will the implementation process be managed, and what integrations are required?

- **Adoption:** How can you ensure quick and comprehensive adoption of new technology? Again, this is something that needs to be looked at on an ongoing basis in collaboration with users and stakeholders.

- **Evaluation and Optimization:** Understanding the critical measures of success is vital here. Optimization against these criteria again is an ongoing process. Technology is continuously evolving with new releases and features. Understanding how you can continuously improve the performance of your technology is a critical ingredient for success.

Future trends

One of the most challenging aspects of using Work Tech effectively within an organization is the importance of understanding how trends will develop in the future. Nothing stands still at the moment, and decisions about software need to be made with a clear eye on the future. There are three types of trends in Work Tech which employers should be following closely.

Technology trends

The first of these are trends in the technology itself. It is obviously impossible to predict the future accurately, but innovations in Work Tech tends to take the lead from innovations elsewhere in enterprise and consumer technology, so it is possible to get a broad sense of what is coming. Here are some examples of technology trends that are likely to influence the development of Work Tech in the coming years:

Better AI

We talked earlier in the chapter about the difference between artificial narrow intelligence and artificial general intelligence. While the latter is most probably still decades away, this doesn't mean we won't see substantial shifts in sophistication in AI in the short to medium term. As AI improves, we can expect to see better results and more Work Tech user cases.

Practical blockchain

Blockchain was considerably hyped a few years ago as the potential engine behind many people functions, including payroll, L&D and reference checking. The reality didn't live up to the hype in the short term, but this is actually nearly always the case when it comes to significant trends in technology. Blockchain has not gone away, and technology analyst firm Gartner had this to say about it in terms of its future use for enterprise applications:

> In the future, true blockchain or "blockchain complete" will have
> the potential to transform industries, and eventually the economy, as
> complementary technologies such as AI and the IoT begin to integrate
> alongside blockchain. Blockchain, which is already appearing in
> experimental and small-scope projects will be fully scalable by 2023.[13]

It is highly likely that blockchain will return to be a consideration in Work Tech in the future.

Alternative user interfaces

Virtual and augmented reality are buzzwords that have been bandied about for years when it comes to predictions around the future. Despite the growing popularity of devices like Facebook's standalone Oculus Quest 2, VR has not yet reached the mainstream. However, with so much investment continuing to go into this space from the likes of Apple, Google and Facebook, it would be unwise to write virtual reality off at this stage. Indeed, there is already some use of virtual reality for business training simulations, and there have been some interesting developments in virtual meeting spaces from companies such as Wonder and Virtulab to help users suffering from pandemic-induced Zoom or Teams fatigue. However, the recent cool reception to the Facebook virtual conference space 'Horizon Workspaces' indicates that there may still be a long way to go before we reach the so-called Metaverse, a virtual environment in which it is predicted we will all work, rest and play in the future.

One other type of user interface which has seen vast growth in both sophistication and popularity is voice. Recent data shows that 38% of UK adults owned a smart speaker (Amazon Echo, Google Nest, Apple HomePod etc.) with voice interfaces and voice assistants moving into the consumer mainstream.[14] Although the use of voice interfaces in Work Tech is not something often discussed, there is already a powerful case study that might point to some exciting potential for the future. Over the last few years, Work Tech vendor Paradox.ai have been working with McDonald's to use conversational AI to help automate hourly hiring. One interesting aspect of this has been the development of 'Apply Thru', which allows job seekers to apply for jobs via the Amazon Alexa or Google Assistant voice interfaces.

Market trends

The second type of trend to follow is the Work Tech market. As well as technology-driven innovation, we are also seeing a drive towards consolidation as the larger well-funded vendors buy up their small innovative competitors and better integration between solutions as more customers adopt a tech stack strategy to Work Tech. Although there will be some disruption for some customers, there is no doubt that the trends towards consolidation and integration will dramatically increase the efficiency and value Work Tech offers.

TA Tech Labs is a research organization that closely tracks the development of talent acquisition technology. Recently on the *Recruiting Future* podcast, their managing director Jonathan Kestenbaum made an observation that is applicable across the whole of the Work Tech ecosystem:

> Currently systems are too separate and don't integrate with each other, but as Robotic Process Automation makes its way into the space, things are going to change. If you have a bot that is the communication layer, the medium through which you communicate with me, there's no reason why that bot couldn't take me across the hiring process, integrating with systems and accessing data. RPA is going to cut across the whole ecosystem as an automation and analytics layer.

With this ever-increasing sophistication comes the need for even higher levels of digital literacy within employers. It is very likely that there will be a trend towards more technology specialists within HR, people operations, and in-house talent acquisition teams. We are already seeing it happening with some employers, reflecting the vital strategic importance of getting Work Tech right.

Strategic trends

By far the most important future trends to watch in Work Tech are strategic trends. These are important because they tend to be employer-driven with companies developing innovative people strategies and pushing for the development of technology to support them. Perhaps the most significant strategic trend to watch over the next few years is the move towards using technology to highly personalize the candidate and employer experience. We have already seen the importance of a high-quality experience to attract and retain digital talent; making this experience an ultra-personalized one is the logical next step.

Technology offers the opportunity to deliver personalization at scale, and we are already starting to see early moves towards this in some aspects of Work Tech. Some examples of this include careers site system vendor Attrax which offers clients the ability to automatically personalize career site content based on user preferences and behaviour. Assessment provider SHL can now give automated personalized video feedback to every candidate who completes one of their assessments. We already see a high degree of personalization within learning management systems, offering personalized learning and career development. The true power of personalization will arrive when these types of solutions are chained together. For example, in talent acquisition, combining the targeting of programmatic advertising, the engagement of a career site system (complete with a friction-free application process), an individually tailored assessment experience and personalized feedback would give the kind of adaptive candidate experience that brings the ultimate competitive advantage.

There are certainly challenges along the way, particularly regarding privacy, but the momentum to personalization is growing. In the past, it has taken a decade or more for significant tech trends such as cloud computing, mobile and social media to be fully assimilated into HR and talent acquisition. With the pandemic now driving change at an unprecedented rate, the road towards the ultimate personalized Work Tech experience will likely be much shorter.

Chapter summary

Effective Work Tech is critical to attract, retain and develop digital talent. AI, automation and more sophistication in the use of data are the key trends every employer needs to be embracing. The market is complex, meaning employers need to take an informed, strategic approach to Work Tech. As demonstrated in this chapter:

- Investment in Work Tech is at record levels and is driving innovation faster than employers can manage adoption.
- Automation is inevitable in all aspects of talent acquisition and HR. Finding the right balance between automation and human interaction will be critical.

- AI is the biggest trend in Work Tech and offers the potential to revolutionize talent acquisition, talent management, learning and development and mobility.

- Transparency and education are critical to making sure AI is implemented and used in an effective, ethical way.

- Data underpins AI and automation. Data-driven platforms are set to revolutionize talent acquisition.

- Personalization is the biggest strategic trend that we will see in Work Tech over the next five years.

Endnotes

1 B Huling. Better Functioning Tech Makes for Less Stress at Work, DELL Technologies, 1 December 2020. www.delltechnologies.com/en-us/blog/blog-better-functioning-tech-makes-for-less-stress-at-work/ (archived at https://perma.cc/XUQ4-YPCC)

2 J Bersin. HR Technology 2021 Now Published: Shattering Changes In The Market, 16 March 2021. https://joshbersin.com/2021/03/hr-technology-2021-now-published-shattering-changes-in-the-market/ (archived at https://perma.cc/L386-UYH6)

3 M Butler. Explaining AI in Recruiting (Part 1), *Recruiting Future* Podcast with Matt Alder, (podcast) recruitingfuture.com/2019/09/ep-207-explaining-ai-in-recruiting-part-1/ (archived at https://perma.cc/78M9-67DA)

4 M Alder. Explaining AI in Recruiting (Part 2), *Recruiting Future* Podcast with Matt Alder, 6 September 2019. recruitingfuture.com/2019/09/ep-208-explaining-ai-in-recruiting-part-2/ (archived at https://perma.cc/8R68-59FT)

5 M Bogen, A Rieke. Help Wanted: An Examination of Hiring Algorithms, Equity, and Bias, Upturn, www.upturn.org/static/reports/2018/hiring-algorithms/files/Upturn%20--%20Help%20Wanted%20-%20An%20Exploration%20of%20Hiring%20Algorithms,%20Equity%20and%20Bias.pdf (archived at https://perma.cc/M4E4-373K)

6 M Alder. Driving Diversity with AI, *Recruiting Future* Podcast with Matt Alder, 4 December 2020. recruitingfuture.com/2020/12/ep-319-driving-diversity-with-ai/ (archived at https://perma.cc/35Y2-6X63)

7 CIPD. People Analytics, 24 May 2021. www.cipd.co.uk/knowledge/strategy/analytics/factsheet#gref (archived at https://perma.cc/G3PJ-M2VK)

8 K Wiggers. SAP acquires AI-powered human resources platform SwoopTalent, Venture Beat, 16 August 2021. venturebeat.com/2021/08/16/sap-acquires-ai-powered-human-resources-platform-swooptalent/ (archived at https://perma.cc/2ZBR-7HNV)

9 SHL. Innovation Rising – the 6 shifts to create an exceptional candidate experience, Unleash Group io, 8 June 2021. www.unleashgroup.io/2021/06/08/innovation-rising-the-six-shifts-creating-exceptional-candidate-experiences/ (archived at https://perma.cc/M4RQ-LUVC)

10 A L Dennis. Data Literacy Leads to Success, *Dataversity*, 11 February 2020, www.dataversity.net/data-literacy-leads-to-success/ (archived at https://perma.cc/A22Q-48A5)

11 WEF. The Future of Jobs Report 2020, www.weforum.org/reports/the-future-of-jobs-report-2020 (archived at https://perma.cc/M92E-V54S)

12 C Boulton. What is RPA? A revolution in business process automation, CIO, 4 September 2018. www.cio.com/article/3236451/what-is-rpa-robotic-process-automation-explained.html (archived at https://perma.cc/34QQ-YFF9)

13 K Panetta. Gartner Top 10 Strategic Technology Trends For 2020, 21 October 2019. www.gartner.com/smarterwithgartner/gartner-top-10-strategic-technology-trends-for-2020/ (archived at https://perma.cc/LR52-DGD7)

14 B Kinsella. BUK Smart Speaker Adoption Surpasses U.S. in 2020, Voicebot.ai, 18 June 2021. voicebot.ai/2021/06/18/uk-smart-speaker-adoption-surpasses-u-s-in-2020-new-report-with-33-charts/ (archived at https://perma.cc/C4KB-KAAP)

08

The new future of work

Predicting the future

Accurately predicting the future is impossible. In his highly influential 2007 book *The Black Swan: The Impact of The Highly Improbable*, author Nassim Nicholas Taleb sets out his black swan theory that history is shaped by events that are hugely influential but also highly unexpected. It would be very easy to see the global COVID 19 pandemic and the huge changes to the world of work it has brought with it as a black swan event that no one could have predicted or planned for. If that is the case, then writing a chapter on the future of work would be a futile exercise.

The unprecedented times we have been living through are not a black swan event. Taleb himself actually describes the global pandemic as a 'white swan event'[1] that was predictable and potentially preventable, at least in terms of the scale of its spread. We'll leave this particular debate to the epidemiologists. Still, when it comes to the effect the pandemic has had on work and the workplace, it is undoubtedly a case of the acceleration of existing trends rather than manifesting the unpredictable.

While we can't accurately predict the actual future, identifying and tracking the trends that will make it is a highly valid way to plan and prepare. The impact of the COVID-19 pandemic has been dramatic, but while there have been some surprises, nothing that has happened in the workplace has been entirely unexpected. What was unpredictable was the speed at which change was forced to happen. So, what does the future of work now look like, what are the implications for digital talent, and what should employers be doing to prepare?

COVID-19, how it changed work for many people, the economic shock and the subsequent labour market shortages worldwide have also driven colossal change. The demand for digital talent was acute before, but the acceleration in digital transformation has made employers' challenges even harder. Ten years' worth of evolution in areas such as remote working, the relationship between employees and employers and the role of automation have happened in fewer than 18 months. The consequences of such a fast and dramatic leap forward are proving to be significant. Employers find themselves with substantial unresolved questions about where work happens, how work happens and what their strategies should be to access the digital skills they need. The next few years are likely to be dynamic, disruptive and potentially chaotic as the business world attempts to find a new equilibrium.

This chapter will look in detail at some of the trends, forces and debates that are now shaping the future of work. What will the workplace look like, what are the vast-reaching implications of automation, and how can we fix the digital skills imbalance?

What next for the workplace?

There is a strong consensus among the many practitioners and thought leaders that we have spoken to in researching this book that the COVID-19 pandemic has accelerated the adoption of remote work by up to a decade. Although it had been a growing trend for knowledge workers for many years, the actual percentage of people working from home or a location outside of the office on a regular basis was very small. In 2019 the Office for National Statistics in the UK reported that only 12.4% of the workforce had worked from home during the week before it conducted its annual national population survey.[2] There is a perception that during the COVID lockdowns of 2020 and 2021, the vast majority of the population (certainly in the UK) worked from home; however, in reality, the percentage of the working population who were doing at least some work at home during the 2020 lockdown actually reached around 47%. There were also strong regional variations between various areas of the country, with London seeing the highest proportion of home workers. Although this percentage fell back to 27%[3] as the lockdown was eased during the summer of 2020, this is still a massive increase from the numbers seen.

Unsurprisingly, remote working was more prevalent in the technology industries. In a survey carried out by Hays in November 2020, 63% of technology professionals said they expected to continue working remotely in the future.[4] While the debate may be less clear cut in other areas, it is clear that the future of the office is a particularly significant issue for employers when it comes to digital talent. It is clear that remote working has some huge advantages both for employees and employers. Many employees have reported a better work-life balance with the lack of commuting time, giving them time back to spend with their families. For employers, it opened up the opportunity of tapping into broader geographic talent pools and, despite dire predictions to the contrary, many found that overall productivity improved. As well, with companies forced to move the entire workforce to remote working in a matter of days with very little pre-planning, the pandemic response has shown employers how quickly they can actually implement major changes. This could well have significant implications for the speed at which companies innovate and manage change moving forward, now that a precedent has been set.

There have also been some considerable disadvantages to remote working. It is important, though, to distinguish between issues caused by remote work and those caused by remote working in a pandemic. The increased stresses caused by pandemic driven issues, such as homeschooling and concerns about physical health and enforced isolation, can cloud the thinking around the future of remote work.

However, there are genuine challenges. Technologies and working practices that weren't designed for a remote workforce have caused huge issues as employees have become burnt out by back-to-back video meetings as employers have attempted to replicate the rhythms and communication styles of the physical workplace in digital form.

There has also been concern about the effect on younger people in the workplace who have not had the opportunity to learn skills in the same immersive way that they had been able to when everyone was physically present in the same place. Many companies have also found it challenging to maintain their working cultures, and many managers have struggled to motivate and develop their teams remotely.

However, many of these issues reflect the incredible speed at which the move to remote working took place. It is pretty certain that working practices, technology and strategies around culture and training will ultimately develop to catch up with the remote working reality. There is a strong possibility that we may well be at the start of a work revolution that changes things forever. Speaking on the *Recruiting Future* Podcast, Rebecca Seal journalist and author of the book *Solo: How to Work Alone* recently shared her optimism for positive change:

> I think we will at least see some organizations who realize that they can have a more human-centred approach to their operations... In the 200 odd years since the end of the industrial revolution, we've been working in patterns that are reflective of what 19th-century industrialists wanted their factory workers to follow that were really only generated by the introduction of electric[al] lighting. We're following modes of working 9 to 5 and 8 hour working days that were never designed to suit the human brain or the human body or human lives. Those things are now being torn up, and the outcome could be something quite brilliant and spectacular. A shift away from ways of working, which for many, many, many people were never suitable in the first place.

The opening up of talent markets that remote working facilitates is also a major benefit and something that will allow employers to compete in a much bigger market for the talent they are looking for. Although ultimately, if other measures are not taken to broaden talent pools by training more people with digital skills, there will still be winners and losers. Remote talent pools may be bigger, but they also come with more competition for talent from a broader geographical base of employers.

It is also important not to ignore the economic and social problems that a whole scale move to remote work will cause. In our research for this book, we spoke to Neil Morrison, Group HR Director at Severn Trent PLC. Severn Trent Water has been championing a highly inclusive approach to talent acquisition and has been named as one of the UK's top companies for helping social mobility. Neil feels strongly that there should be a 'regional dispersal of industries and businesses so that people can live in their communities and work in those businesses'. He points out that well-paid city workers are using their salaries which reflect the expense of city living to buy up properties in more rural areas, displacing the local population and stifling opportunities to improve social mobility. Inequality of home working environment is another crucial issue that Neil identifies:

> One of the things that, that I think we've seen, during the last year, is that your ability to work at home effectively depends on the facilities that you've got there. Many people have been forced to work on the corner of their kitchen table because they don't have a spare room that can be turned into a study. So there is an economic background to this as well. One of the first things that we noticed is that not everybody's home working environment is equal, so from that perspective, there are some real challenges.

There are still many unknown factors about the mass adoption of home working: the effect on population distribution and impact on city centre economies are just two of them. There could be some severe economic and social challenges ahead as the world transitions to new ways of working. Ultimately though, employers wanting to have the best digital talent in their organizations may not have a choice. In 2021, survey after survey indicated that a majority of employees wish to continue to work remotely. We have already seen that 63% of technology professionals expect to stay remote. Recent Harvard Business Review research found that nearly 80% of US employees wanted to work from home at least some of the time.[5]

Many people have now been working from home for the best part of two years, forming new habits and establishing new norms. Employers cannot expect their employees to unquestioningly return to the office as if nothing has happened. The consequences of a forced return in such tight labour markets are likely to be severe both for talent retention and talent acquisition. Even companies with the strongest employer brand aren't immune. Apple regularly tops surveys as the employer people most want to work for. Despite this, their plans to require employees to work in the office three days a week have generated significant pushback and negative publicity. Some employees feel that views on the continuation of remote work have been ignored.[6]

There are also critical issues here around diversity and inclusion. The evidence clearly points to the importance of flexibility in attracting and retaining a diverse workforce. The *Harvard Business Review* research previously cited also revealed a desire for more work from home time from university-educated women with children. Workforce culture expert Bruce Daisley recently wrote about this in a newsletter article titled 'Offices are a battlefront for equality'. Reflecting on 12 months of enforced remote work, he noted that 'There is a privilege in being able to travel miles to reach a desk for 9 am and to leave it at 6 pm. It is a privilege that if it doesn't relax to accommodate childcare or the realities of modern life, immediately becomes an invisible barrier to a more diverse workforce.'[7]

The changing relationship between employee and employer

If we are living through a time of seismic change around the way work works, a key part of this is the reappraisal of the relationship between employer and employee, and this is something that is particularly critical when it comes to digital talent. COVID-19 has forced people to reappraise the work they do and why they do it, and the talent shortages we see in many areas have empowered them to make their voices heard.

In a recent episode of the *Recruiting Future* podcast, Rory Sutherland, vice chairman at Ogilvy and one of the world's leading experts on applying behavioural science in business, highlighted the problem in traditional business thinking:

> I don't think it's unhealthy for companies actually to start thinking, how do we keep people? How do we look after them? Can we make the relationship between employer and employee a bit less transactional? Because the assumption that my job was infinitely replaceable by hungry people coming from elsewhere had an unintended side effect of making labour economics ridiculously transactional. You turn up and don't cock up. We'll give you some money this month, but don't think we're committed to you in the long term, medium term because we don't care…I would argue that employment is immensely relational; it's way out on that scale. Yet labour economics effectively says, the reason your pay is called compensation is because it compensates you for a loss of leisure, it is very much focused on that totally crude question of transactional exchange.

Unsurprisingly then the momentum for change is building. In the summer of 2021, McKinsey conducted interviews with 70 European CHROs and found a strong shift towards more people-centric policies. So 90% of interviewees had a focus on 'Engage more directly and deeply with employees' and 98% had a focus on 'Let employees bring their whole person to work'.[8]

The precise future for the workplace does, though, remain uncertain. Some employers have taken an early decision to call time on compulsory office attendance. Technology unicorn Canva has very much left the decision up to its employees and only now requires them to be in the office for eight days a year.[9] Other companies have been even bolder; Atlassian, for example, has implemented a 'Team Anywhere' policy which allows its 5,700 staff to work from anywhere in the world and only mandates them to come to the office four times a year.[10]

The way forward

For most employers, though, deciding on a way forward is difficult. There has been much focus on creating hybrid working patterns that allow employees to work remotely some of the time and in the office some of the time. There is an intention here to get the best of both worlds and avoid the disadvantages and negatives of both. However, there are huge question marks about how this will work in practice and significant logistical issues around how much office space is required and who comes to the office when. Employers also have to go to considerable lengths to persuade people back to the office, offering free food and various other incentives to tempt their employees back. Perhaps the biggest issue here is the attempt to design compromise solutions that end up not working well for anyone. Ultimately, there can be nothing more disheartening than commuting to an office in anticipation of face-to-face interaction only to spend all day on video calls with colleagues who are working remotely that day. Rory Sutherland highlights the issue of optimizing for the average as a long-term problem in office design:

> I hate open-plan offices because I think they're neither one thing nor the other. They're an attempt to solve for the average. Actually, what you want for productivity is two extremes, a mixture of solitude and sociability. You also need a mixture of very high-intensity work, concentrated work and periods of discretionary free time. What generally leads to productivity in a knowledge economy is actually a highly varied working environment. Bear in mind, in addition, that the role of the office will be completely different for different people. Some people will now be going to the office to escape the chaos that is their home life, and some people were going to the office because they're bored and lonely at home and actually want to have a bit of noise and chat and banter.

> So any attempt to optimize for an average is a fatal mistake in any complex system. What you want is an optimal level of variance, non-optimal average. The question should not be what is the perfect working environment to impose on everybody for 35 hours a week.

It should be, what's the optimal variety we need to provide people with so they can find an environment that best suits their own cognitive style which suits what they're trying to do in the moment.

So how should employers be thinking? Pagaya's chief people officer Tami Rosen, who has helped design distributed work strategies for a number of organizations, shared these thoughts on the *Recruiting Future* Podcast:

> There are three elements that people need to think about as they design their programs.
>
> One is how we help employees customize their work routines that fits best with both their professional and personal lives, and create harmony between the two, so they can work best and be most productive.
>
> The second piece is all about talent reach. In the past, we've been bounded by the physical office spaces. Now, you can access talent everywhere and really increase the diversity of talent you have to support your team and mission.
>
> The third piece is to find collaborative moments where you can intentionally collaborate both digitally and also in person. Intentional moments of togetherness are powerful to help teams build connection, trust, and empathy.
>
> I do believe more and more tech companies are moving towards a distributed and flexible environment. I think they're taking that leap because COVID has changed our thinking on how and where we work, showing us we can be productive from anywhere.

There is a long way to go here, with many failed policies and pilots to come before we can have any proper sense of what the future might look like. However, what is very clear is that employees now hold the power and any company that is serious about wanting to recruit, retain and develop digital talent for their organization needs to listen closely to its employees and the people in external talent pools it is targeting.

Fixing the skills imbalance

The future of the labour market is precarious. The World Economic Forum predicted in 2020 that 85 million jobs would be lost to automation by 2025. It is likely that COVID-19 is further accelerating this as companies seek to fill gaps caused by a lack of available talent to speed up their journey towards automation. There is also the issue of building business resilience against other unexpected future events and some companies will see a strategy that reduces their reliance on a human workforce as a way to do this. It is important to say that digital transformation and automation also create jobs, and the WEF predicts that these changes in the way we work will actually create 97 million new jobs. However, the crux of the issue is that the jobs being created need different skills from those they are replacing. The jobs most at risk from automation are those that focus on repeatable tasks. The WEF includes occupations as diverse as accountants, customer service professionals, general managers and mechanics on its at risk of automation list. Unsurprisingly, the jobs being created have a strong digital focus and include roles in areas such as data, AI, software engineering and digital strategy.[11] Fixing the skills imbalance between those being displaced and the requirements of the roles being created is critical.

Skills for the future workforce

The role of schools and universities in equipping their students with the right skills to survive and thrive in the ever-changing digital world is vital. As we have seen throughout this book, it isn't just STEM skills that are needed but the cultivation of digital mindsets, flexible thinking and the entrepreneurial drive that will enable the workforce of the future to cope with an ever-increasing pace of disruptive change. Unfortunately, though, this seems to be a role that education systems in many countries are failing in.

We've already seen that despite the UK government's re-invention of computer science qualifications to make them more relevant, in

2018 only 11.9% of students were taking computer science at GCSE and 2.7% at A-Level. Sadly, this isn't just a UK issue and is a pattern repeated throughout the rest of Europe. A recent European Commission survey of 85,000 headteachers, teachers, students and parents from the EU's member states as well as Norway, Iceland and Turkey revealed that over 70% of secondary school students never or 'almost never' engage in coding or programming at school.[12] The picture is similar elsewhere in the world; a recent report for the Australia Industry Group[13] pointed to a declining trend in ICT skills in schools and a declining take up from students of STEM-related studies in science and maths. In the USA, a recent survey of school educators by PWC revealed that 64% of teachers felt there should be more emphasis on teaching technology, and 79% wanted more professional development to help them teach technology-related subjects.[14] While it is important for employers all over the world to put pressure on governments to ensure that digital inclusion and literacy skills are a priority, this is not a quick or easy solution to the problem. So what else could companies be doing to ensure a future supply of talent with the skills and mindset that is needed?

James Uffindell is the founder and CEO of The Bright Network, an organization with a mission to connect its over half a million students with the best careers using data and technology; it has a strong focus on diversity. Their research and work with students and employers shine a spotlight on the issues of equipping the future workforce with the digital skills they need. As James says:

> Schools and colleges should be doing more to equip young people with the right skills to thrive in a digital economy. Whilst traditional subject knowledge is important, the importance of technical, digital education is overlooked in the UK education system.

> The job market is rapidly evolving with an estimated 800 million jobs disappearing in the near future at the hands of AI and other emerging technologies – these jobs will be replaced with different roles that require an understanding of new technologies and the ability to utilize them.

Our 2019 survey found that 32% of graduates feel they need to upskill in coding and 29% in Core IT skills, before entering the world of work. This shows that the current education system is not adequately preparing young people with the skills they need to prepare for the jobs of today, let alone the jobs of tomorrow. It is essential that schools put more emphasis on digital education – IT and coding need to be put properly onto the core curriculum. The curriculum needs to be able to adapt to change, evolving as the job market evolves.

In addition to this, creativity also forms part of the digital job market with a multitude of opportunities in fields such as advertising, design and media. It is vital that career guidance advises students on where their creative skills can fit into the digital economy. It is not just about technical education; it is also about educating humanities and art students about how they can contribute and succeed in the changing job market.

Although governments and educators have a pivotal part to play, James also believes that the role of employers is absolutely critical:

Employers from the tech industry need to take on an even greater role in supporting students. They should have a vested interest in ensuring the new generation of workers are attracted to the industry and can achieve this by collaborating with schools and colleges.

There are clear steps that tech leaders can take. By introducing digital skills workshops, encouraging entrepreneurial skills, visiting local schools and promoting commercial awareness, employers can work with schools to equip students for success as well as building their talent pipeline.

James also emphasizes the importance of employers taking an active role in supporting students as they make their career decisions:

Businesses can play a key role in improving careers guidance in educational institutions in a number of ways including giving informative talks to students about the various opportunities that lie beyond education and offering work experience programmes to students.

While the onus is on governments to set policies around education and provide support for retraining, it is clear that there is also a significant responsibility on employers to help fix the problem.

One company taking this very seriously at a global level is Tata Consultancy Services (TCS), a large multi-national company with 450,000 employees. TCS runs a number of programmes to support the development of STEM skills with schools all over the world. 'goIT' is an experiential and immersive student technology awareness programme running in schools across Europe and North America to help inspire the workforce of the future. The programme has engaged over 10,000 students so far, with 70% reporting a great interest in STEM fields after the programme.[15]

One of the other programmes TCS runs is even more ambitious in scale. 'Ignite My Future In School'[16] offers educators in the US free resources to empower them to integrate the teaching of computational thinking into core subjects such as English, maths, science, art and social science. TCS pitches computational thinking as taking into account '21st-century technology and overlaps it with key strategies to solve any given challenge'. They believe that by 'teaching students to solve problems using the same components as a computer, we prepare them for bright futures where they can combine creativity with computational thinking for ultimate innovation and success'. Ignite My Future In School has already reached over 670,000 students via over 11,600 educators in the US schools' system.

Upskilling the current workforce

While ensuring the future workforce has access to appropriate resources to help them find future jobs is critically important, upskilling the existing workforce with digital skills is now urgent. During the COVID-19 pandemic, training and upskilling have become a priority for many organizations. The 2021 McKinsey Skills Survey reported that companies were prioritizing skill-building, with 69% of respondents saying they were doing more than before the pandemic began.[17] There was also a 16-percentage point increase in the number of companies making basic digital skills a priority than in the same survey carried out in 2019.

However, if employers want a truly competitive advantage when it comes to digital talent, then the focus on upskilling needs to go beyond their existing workforces. This is somewhere where the rapid acceleration in the innovation of work tech and the trend towards building longer-term pipelines of talent could combine to deliver a competitive advance for companies progressive enough to take it. Long-term talent pipelining only works with appropriate high-quality engagement. What better to drive engagement and increase the quality of the pipeline than to offer training? This is something that could be delivered by specific development initiatives, or alternatively, employees could grant potential hires broader access to internal digital learning platforms.

Total talent thinking

Whichever direction the future of work heads, it is evident that employers will need to think differently to secure digital talent. It is also crystal clear that there isn't a single solution to the challenge. Digital talent will remain scarce for years to come, and employers will need to implement various strategies simultaneously to have the right skills in their business to meet their needs. With that in mind, it is likely that the demand for digital talent within an organization will be met with a combination of internal mobility, L&D, talent acquisition and accessing contingent and on-demand workforces.

Marketplaces for talent are already evolving to support the concept of on-demand working, and this is likely to be a strong trend for the future. Tim Pröhm, vice president of Digital Product Architecture at staffing firm Kelly, is already seeing the development of what he refers to as the Human Cloud:

> when you take a look at the existing operating model, in talent acquisition, and in the staffing industry, there is a real disconnect[ion] between talent and the organization. So, you might promote your jobs, advertise your jobs, somebody might find you, or you might require

an agency to do the job for you because you didn't have an inside view into what talent is available in the market. I feel that with the emergence of talent marketplaces, there is much more visibility. You have an understanding of who is available in the marketplace, even outside of your country. These human cloud platforms could have millions of candidate records. I find somebody, I sent that person a note and they respond in a couple of minutes, maybe half an hour, and it's much more real-time than the traditional staffing processes are. I think that's something where a lot of organizations and a lot of hiring managers will see the benefit and really push to engage with these platforms much more.

The advances in AI technology are already presenting companies with the solutions they need to manage a broader approach to talent strategy. In the previous chapter, we explored how AI was already being used to power internal mobility. In the near future, AI solutions will work across internal and external talent pools to provide employers with the right skills at the right time. Vendors like Eightfold are already working towards this kind of vision; offering AI-powered 'talent intelligence platforms' that create job architectures based on skills and abilities that work internally and externally to the organization.

In his brilliant book, *The End of Jobs*, Jeff Wald, a serial entrepreneur and the co-founder of WorkMarket, sets out a vision for the 'agile corporation', companies using technology to access on-demand talent. He suggests that total talent management will see companies breaking work down into specific tasks and managing all of their labour resources (which might include freelancers, employees, robots and drones) in a single platform:

> This is the future of work… This is how companies are using data, mobile, machine learning, APIs, algorithms, and AI to optimize their workforce. This is how companies can operate in a flexible, agile structure and compete in any economic environment.

Perhaps the biggest issue around these talent markets that will drive the future of work is equity in the treatment of workers, whether they are permanent employees or not. With the advent of so-called gig working platforms like Uber and Deliveroo, we have already seen legal battles in several countries over workers' employment status and rights. During the COVID-19 pandemic, we saw huge issues with certain types of freelancers struggling to get any kind of financial support from the UK government because they paid tax through limited company set-ups rather than PAYE. These are the kind of legal, regulatory and policy challenges that are set to intensify as on-demand working makes the whole notion of employment more opaque. The onus is on companies to do the right thing by their workers, whatever terms they employ them under. In late 2021 Google hit the headlines when it came to light that they had been knowingly and illegally underpaying thousands of temporary workers around the world for years.[18] Big technology companies are now very much under the spotlight for treating freelance workers as a secondary workforce with worse pay and conditions than full-time workers doing the same job.

As employers move to total talent management solutions and increase their reliance on freelancer workers, it will be in their commercial interests to treat all of their workers the same way. Employer brands won't just be something that are leveraged to attract the permanent staff; they will be relevant for everyone who works for the organization, even if that work is just one short term project. In the workplace of the future, whether it is remote, in-person or hybrid, a company's reputation as an employer will have a significant impact on its ability to attract and retain digital talent.

Chapter summary

This is a hugely disruptive time, and we will see new models for work and the workplace emerging over the next few years. The digital skills gap will get bigger, and employers need to take an active role in helping to close it. As we've discussed in this chapter:

• Remote or partly remote workforces offer the opportunity to access broader pools of digital talent but may limit the ability to train and upskill younger workers.

- The relationship between employees and employers has changed from transactional to relational and employees currently have the power.

- Technology offers the opportunity to adopt a total talent management approach to ensure organizations have access to the digital skills they need. Employers need to look at a combination of recruiting, internal mobility, upskilling and a contingent / on-demand workforce.

- AI offers the opportunity to create just-in-time internal and external talent marketplaces.

- Equity in the treatment of workers regardless of their employment status will be vital for competitive talent advantage.

Endnotes

1 Bloomberg. Nassim Taleb Says 'White Swan' Coronavirus Pandemic Was Preventable (online video) 30 March 2020. www.bloomberg.com/news/videos/2020-03-30/nassim-taleb-says-white-swan-coronavirus-pandemic-was-preventable-video (archived at https://perma.cc/T7FY-RYQX)

2 R Partington. Most people in the UK did not work from home in 2020, says ONS, *The Guardian*, 17 May 2021. www.theguardian.com/world/2021/may/17/home-working-doubled-during-uk-covid-pandemic-last-year-mostly-in-london (archived at https://perma.cc/6XHE-KPE6)

3 Office for National Statistics. Working from Home: comparing the data, 17 May 2021, blog.ons.gov.uk/2021/05/17/working-from-home-comparing-the-data/ (archived at https://perma.cc/4DUH-4DYK)

4 S Ranger. Remote Work is Here to Stay. Tech workers are Starting to Worry About Their Careers, ZDNet, 7 October 2020. www.zdnet.com/article/remote-work-is-here-to-stay-tech-workers-are-starting-to-worry-about-their-careers/ (archived at https://perma.cc/6S6V-TSCQ)

5 J M Barrero, N Bloom, S J Davis. *Harvard Business Review*. Don't force people to come back to the office full time?, 24 August 2021. https://hbr.org/2021/08/dont-force-people-to-come-back-to-the-office-full-time (archived at https://perma.cc/BH8M-4Z6F)

6 Z Schiffer. Apple Employees Push Back Against Returning to the Office in Internal Letter, *The Verge*, 4 June 2021. www.theverge.com/2021/6/4/22491629/apple-employees-push-back-return-office-internal-letter-tim-cook (archived at https://perma.cc/G2PR-D38B)

7 Make Work Better. Offices are a battleground for equality, 16 March 2021. makeworkbetter.substack.com/p/offices-are-a-battlefront-for-equality (archived at https://perma.cc/5HTV-YSKF)

8 T Khan, A Komm, D Maor and F Pollner. Back to human: Why HR leaders want to focus on people again, McKinsey & Company, 4 June 2021, www.mckinsey.com/business-functions/organization/our-insights/back-to-human-why-hr-leaders-want-to-focus-on-people-again?utm_campaign=Recruiting%20Brainfood&utm_medium=email&utm_source=Revue%20newsletter (archived at https://perma.cc/3NNH-86FZ)

9 B Healey. Traditional Workplaces Will Become The Exception: Canva Says Employees Will Only Need To Come To The Office 8 Times A Year, Business Insider Australia, 31 August 2021. www.businessinsider.com.au/canva-new-flexible-work-policy (archived at https://perma.cc/V46P-KLJT)

10 T Khan, A Komm, D Maor and F Pollner. Back to human: Why HR leaders want to focus on people again, McKinsey & Company, 4 June 2021, www.mckinsey.com/business-functions/organization/our-insights/back-to-human-why-hr-leaders-want-to-focus-on-people-again?utm_campaign=Recruiting%20Brainfood&utm_medium=email&utm_source=Revue%20newsletter (archived at https://perma.cc/3DJY-B5J4)

11 World Economic Forum, The Future of Jobs Report 2020, www.weforum.org/reports/the-future-of-jobs-report-2020 (archived at https://perma.cc/D2M6-HKE5)

12 Tech Monitor. Over 70% of EU Students Never Code at School, techmonitor.ai/techonology/data-centre/code-week-eu (archived at https://perma.cc/DD6P-P7PD)

13 AI Group. Developing the Workforce for a Digital Future, cdn.aigroup.com.au/Reports/2018/Developing_the_workforce_for_a_digital_future.pdf (archived at https://perma.cc/EC4W-9UL9)

14 PWC. Responsible Business Leadership in Focus, www.pwc.com/us/en/about-us/corporate-responsibility/library/preparing-students-for-technology-jobs.html (archived at https://perma.cc/2XFR-USC4)

15 TATA Consultancy Services. The TCS goIT Student Technology Awareness Program inspires the workforce of the future, www.tcs.com/tcs-goit-student-technology-awareness-program (archived at https://perma.cc/T28R-C765)

16 TATA Sustainability Group (2021) Ignite My Future in School (IMFIS), www.tatasustainability.com/SocialAndHumanCapital/IgniteMyFutureInSchool (archived at https://perma.cc/C96V-WEAU)

17 McKinsey & Company. Building workforce skills at scale to thrive during–and after–the COVID-19 crisis, 30 April 2021. www.mckinsey.com/business-functions/organization/our-insights/building-workforce-skills-at-scale-to-thrive-during-and-after-the-covid-19-crisis?cid=other-eml-nsl-mip-mck&hlkid=ccd4a3a2990c44599c5f479309f4403c&hctky=12222495&hdpid=87cae261-a7ce-4c1d-805c-7f1c544f8d10 (archived at https://perma.cc/R7Z3-92FD)

18 M Sainato. A race to the bottom: Google temps are fighting a two-tier labour system, *The Guardian*, 24 September 2021. www.theguardian.com/technology/2021/sep/24/google-temps-fighting-two-tier-labor-system (archived at https://perma.cc/4FT4-FEHM)

Conclusion

The digital talent journey

With every month and year that goes by, the demand for digital skills from employers intensifies. The situation was challenging before the global pandemic, but events since 2020 have accelerated the imbalance between the demand and supply of digital talent to a damaging level for many employers as they attempt to digitally transform their businesses. Governments are finally starting to wake up to the problem, particularly as the rise in automation starts to displace people from their jobs. However, initiatives to retrain redundant workers and ensure the education systems are correctly resourced to produce future digital talent at any kind of scale will take the time that many businesses don't have. To ensure they have the right digital skills to drive digital transformation, employers will have to adopt a total talent management mindset that incorporates permanent hiring, the use of contingent workforces, as well as talent development and internal mobility. HR must use data and technology to transform themselves into anticipators armed with the people analytics and insights to forecast the skills and capabilities their business will need in the future. Companies also need to develop inclusive cultures and work with their employees to generate a sense of purpose that everyone can share across the entire workforce, regardless of whether they are permanent employees or talented individuals from outside the organization bringing their skills to specific short-term projects.

So, what kind of strategic thinking is needed for employers to achieve this kind of talent transformation? In our previous book, *Exceptional Talent*, we set out a six-stage circular model, which we argued was essential for employers to acquire and retain the very best people for their business. At the crux of everything was the notion of the joined-up talent experience we have been talking about in this book. Historically it has been difficult for organizations to adopt this kind of approach with barriers such as internal silos, rigid processes and a lack of integration between technology platforms that have stood in the way.

What we are seeing from employers now is that the COVID-19 pandemic has been a catalyst for what could amount to revolutionary change. The initial shock of lockdown, and a freezing up of economies, made companies think hard about internal mobility as they dealt with the dual threat of potential headcount reduction and acute need for digital skills, while 7 years' worth of digital transformation happened in 12 months. Lockdowns and forced remote working gave knowledge workers and businesses new impetus to reflect on the future of work and the nature of the employee/employer relationship. The removal of the daily commute also opened up new geographic talent pools, which many employers continue to take advantage of. As economies began to open up again, we saw the realities of the much-heralded 'great resignation' as employees who had been biding their time during the stress of the pandemic looked for new opportunities. Talent markets went crazy, and talent acquisition once more found itself in the spotlight, looking for new and innovative strategies and tactics to get a competitive advantage.

Against this background, billions of dollars have been invested in technology as HR technology morphs into work tech. With the rise of AI, automation, and increasing sophistication in the collection and use of data, we are beginning to see more focus on integration and interoperability between tech vendors. We finally see technology stacks that can deliver the kind of total talent management companies now need.

Implementing an integrated, connected talent journey is more essential than ever. The changes we have seen in the way companies are thinking about it mean that it is more practical to do than ever. Although there are six stages to what we can now call the digital talent journey, it is essential to see things holistically as an evolving, interlocking process that reviews, reinvents and repurposes. As we have described earlier in the book, our potential candidates and employees expect a seamless, integrated journey, much like the one they get as consumers. They want to know where they stand at each stage of the journey and also expect some form of indication or feedback at each step so they can better judge their progress. Historically this may have been a physical journey with a person-to-person interaction at each stage; however, for digital talent this is most definitely a digital journey. Unfortunately, many hiring and talent management processes are designed from the company's viewpoint, streamlining the areas that make it easier for them to attract, evaluate and either reject or hire. This creates a poor experience for candidates and, as we have seen earlier in the book, will often lead to them either exiting the process, or sharing their negative experiences online for others to see, or most often, both.

Here are the four core stages of the digital talent journey that we believe all organizations must pay attention to, ensuring that each stage is intuitive, seamless, informative and effortless to navigate:

Attention and attraction

Getting the attention of digital talent in an intensely competitive market and attracting the right people to the business:

- Digital skills adapt and evolve continuously, and competition is intense. This means that employers need to be flexible in their thinking about how they define their hiring requirements. Potential and mindset will be far more important than current skills and past experience.
- Acquiring experienced digital talent for an organization is a strategic challenge. This is true for both the permanent and contract workforce. Employers need to take a long-term view and build meaningful engagement with their target audience.

Remote working and wider geographical pipelines mean that some of the traditional ways of promoting an employer brand are no longer effective. Understanding the motivations of the target audience and communicating clearly about purpose is essential.

Recruitment and onboarding

This is usually the most crucial stage as it helps determine if digital talent wants to join you, and how well they start their career with you, and is often complicated by having different internal stakeholders.

- Recruitment and onboarding are key opportunities to align the external perception of your talent experience with the internal reality of how you operate. There should be no questions or steps aimed at wrong-footing candidates. Create a process that allows them to showcase what skills and knowledge they can bring to your organization.

- The hiring phase is personal for candidates. Make sure they know where they stand at each stage of the process and give them regular, consistent and actionable feedback on how they are performing and progressing. Candidates should always know where they stand, and what they need to do to progress.

- Start onboarding as early as possible. After the first or second interview, you should effectively be starting the onboarding process. One of the candidates you are taking through the process will be a new employee. The others, who you may have to reject, could become an employee at some stage in the future. Even if they don't, they will be advocates for the quality of your recruitment experience.

- The process of onboarding should be designed to help set new hires up for success. It isn't about the first few days, but about their first three months with your company. Give them all the tools and knowledge they will need to succeed and help them to connect with their new colleagues.

Engagement and development

Creating the right culture and environment in which digital talent can thrive, produce their best work and achieve their personal goals:

- Improve employee engagement through continual, consistent activity, not one-off initiatives.
- Understand the micro-experiences that matter to employees every day, whether they are office-based or remote, and ensure that the number of positive experiences is maximized.
- Create a supportive culture of learning and feedback that enables employees to grow, develop and learn the new skills necessary to move the business forward.
- Empower leaders and managers to use feedback positively and constructively.
- Use talent intelligence to identify the people who will be able to move around the organization, building knowledge and developing skills in different areas of the business.
- Nurture a culture of internal mobility so that digital talent doesn't believe they have to leave the organization in order to achieve their goals.

As our digital talent embraces a more hybrid approach to working that includes both locational flexibility and a desire to balance their work and personal lives, we need to make sure that our remote working tools can support them and can help provide the connections they need with colleagues to collaborate and help produce their best work. Leaders must nurture a real culture of recognition around the whole organization.

Alumni and advocacy

Turning the former workforce into employer brand advocates:

- The talent experience shouldn't finish when someone leaves the organization. Former employees, contractors and gig workers are both a talent pool for re-hiring and an important source of brand equity and referral.

- This can't be left to chance; employers need to actively manage their external reputations by monitoring review sites and building effective engagement strategies with their former employees.

Final thoughts

Hiring, engaging, developing and retaining digital talent has been a challenge for employers since business computing went mainstream in the 1960s. However, over the last 20 years, with the rise of the internet and a massive acceleration in technology innovation, the challenge has increased every year.

During the process of writing this book, the COVID-19 pandemic has accelerated digital transformation and the need for digital talent at a previously unimaginable speed. It is very clear that we are at a tipping point in the work of the world. A growing focus on diversity, equity and inclusion, the disconnection between work and the workplace, a step-change in the relationship between employee and employer and the rise of AI will make the next decade truly transformational.

We have written this book to try and help those working in HR, recruitment and business management to understand the challenges, and the evolving preferences and expectations, of digital talent.

As leaders and managers strive to build their businesses profitably and successfully in the age of digital transformation, we hope that through the research and analysis of current and emerging trends, and advice that we have showcased in this book, we are able to play our part in helping all organizations to grow and thrive in the era of accelerated digital transformation.

INDEX